Advance Praise for *Man Things*

Wholly refreshing. A clever and talented writer, Paine possesses an ability that is apart from the crowd. I laughed myself to tears over chapter 18, "The Crowbar."

> *Tim Walters*
> Executive Editor, Rawhide Western Publishing

This is a masterpiece. A voice America is longing to hear. I'm deeply moved. I couldn't put it down.

> *Gordon Baxter*
> Contributing Editor, FLYING Magazine

Lauran Paine has achieved with *Man Things* for the man about the house, what Erma Bombeck did for the housewife. It follows the development of male bonding, a bonding that takes place between father and son and the possessions and activities that make men what they are. And what they are and how they got there is the essence of what this book is about.
This book is a great read. It is sure to make the perfect gift for that man in your life—or the boy about to become a man!

> *William W. Forgey, M.D.*
> Vice President, Acquisitions, ICS Books, Inc.

This insightful book is sure to bring back memories and feelings of past experiences.

> *Nick Amato*
> Editor, Salmon Trout Steelheader magazine

This is really good.

> *Dave*

BY THE SAME AUTHOR

If Airplanes Could Talk: The Pilot's Book of Wit and Wisdom

Dean,
Happy 50th!
Best Wishes
from
Phil and Wendy

Man Things

* * *

equal time for men

Lauran Paine Jr.

CASCADE PUBLISHING
SALEM, OREGON

Published by Cascade Publishing
P.O. Box 4598, Salem, Oregon 97302

Printed by Maverick Publications
Bend, Oregon

Cover photography © Jill Cannefax
Dayton, Oregon

Paine, Lauran, Jr.
    Man things: equal time for men.
Life—men's issues—humor / Lauran Paine Jr.—1st ed.

ISBN: 0-9657607-3-1 : $12.95 (pbk.)

Library of Congress Catalog Card Number: 97-67125

for my bride of twenty-eight years,
who tolerates, for the most part,
man things

CONTENTS

INTRODUCTION

This is a book about man things, the things men like, think, and do. If you read between the lines, it says a lot about why men act like men. I don't know where I first heard the term, but my wife uses it all the time. Whenever I am doing something that I think is a lot more fun than she does, she says, "Must be a man thing."

The things in this book are not the exclusive domain of men. They are simply described from the man's perspective. I don't pretend to explain every man's inner workings, so take this as a general guideline, somewhat generic, but definitely a view from *inside* man land.

Man things can be both good and bad. Building a fence is a good man thing; being insensitive is a bad man thing. I have tried to write about the good man things. It is more fun that way. It is also safer.

Growing up on a farm and becoming an airline pilot, I have experienced a lot of man things. Much of what I write comes deep from the heart. But I certainly have not experienced them all. I have not built a house, driven an eighteen-wheeler, or operated heavy equipment. So I spent time with men who have. In these pages are their man things. I thank them for sharing.

Do me one favor. When you read the chapters, slow down. Do not let the rush of the day interfere. This is feel good stuff. Read slow. Feel it. Enjoy it. Feel good. That's what this book is all about.

Welcome to the world of man things.

LP

1
UNDER THE HOOD

Under the hood is not just a man thing. It is a man place. You have to have a car or truck to play. The hood has to be up. Then you stand around, with your hands in your pockets, and peer into the engine compartment. An older car is best because there is less stuff you don't recognize. If it is a newer car you still have to act like you recognize everything, or you risk losing your man standing. An occasional, "They don't make 'em like they used to," is somewhat risky, but okay. What that really means is, 'I don't know what half the stuff in here is.' But at least you did not admit it outright. That would not be cool.

Alone under the hood you can actually reach in and touch stuff, trying to figure out where it goes so you can figure out what it does. A little dirt and grime on the hands lends realism to what you are doing. Grime is good. Realism is important.

Three or four men under the hood and the rules change. You mostly have to act like you know what everything is. And you have to know how to fix it or, at least, offer how so-and-so fixed it. In under-the-hood-groupings, talking of fixing and offering advice becomes nearly as important as the actual fixing. Usually very little gets accomplished. It's not supposed to. When everybody leaves, you go back to wondering what made you think you could fix it in the first place. Or more importantly, how to admit to your spouse that you can't fix it. The 'time angle' usually works best. "Big deal goin' on at the office. I'd fix it but just don't have the time right now. Gotta take it to the garage . . . darn it." Or you can always try the 'tool angle.' "Just don't have the right tool. I gotta get me one of those framitz-removers someday."

Occasionally men actually do accomplish something under the hood, like changing the oil. Time is critical to establishing legitimacy to your work. I hate Quickie Lube. They can't do it quick and I can't do it under three hours. Unscrewing the drain plug, draining the oil, screwing the plug back in and then putting in new oil may not seem like a lot, but it is. Like I said, it is a three hour job, done right. Doing it right means talking about it the night before. "Gotta work on the car tomorrow." That usually serves to relieve you of dishwasher emptying and vacuuming. Not always, but usually. When it works it is really slick. You've laid claim to a man thing morning.

Doing it right also means using coveralls and a fender apron and setting out all the stuff . . . oil, wrenches, rags, etc., on the workbench beforehand and reflecting a bit on the task you are about to undertake. Reflecting can be risky. Get caught reflecting too long and you will end up emptying the dishwasher.

You get to work. (The football game comes on in another two hours and you think you can stretch the oil change another two hours.) You place the oil drain pan under the car and unscrew the drain plug. Unscrewing the drain plug is NEVER easy. They are ALWAYS hard to do. You try and do it without getting oil all over your hand and arm but you always get oil all over your hand and arm. All this takes time. You stay under the car. If your wife looks in the garage and all she sees are your legs and feet sticking out, she will generally leave you alone. You are safe in man land. When the last drop of oil has dripped (and you've finished your short nap under the car) you put the oil drain plug back in.

You are now ready to finish the job with a flourish. You put the new oil in. (Secret stalling tactic: check the dip stick after each quart.) Then you clean up. Your timing is good, one-half hour to go. You clean up slow. Then you start the car to 'check it out.' When your wife hears it running she will know you've accomplished your task. Your timing is still good. The game starts soon. You come in and shower, plop down on the couch and grab the remote. The game starts and, whew, you are tired from all that man work. You really deserve the break. You give your wife the 'I-need-the-rest look.' It works. You just earned three hours of couch potato time. Oil change by morning. Football game by afternoon. A perfect man day.

2
HARDWARE STORES

Hardware stores are not in the malls. They are just out there. They are on the edges of towns. Facsimiles or replicas can be found "departmentalized" in the humongous chain stores (HCS's). You can go to the HCS's for a (as in one) tool, but they are not the real thing. No atmosphere.

The real thing is just a hardware store, by itself, in a building by itself, with a sidewalk out front and a partially paved parking lot beside the building. The real thing has a couple of plate glass windows in front with a double screen door between them. Plate glass windows say HARDWARE STORE on them. When you get inside and look out it says EROTS ERAWDRAH.

As you step inside, the well worn hardwood floor creaks a bit. Behind the equally well worn counter stands an elderly gentleman with an apron and glasses on. He has worked at the store for a long time. He knows you. He says something like, "How ya doin? How's the missus?"

You have to wear boots in a hardware store. Worn out athletic shoes are gaining some acceptance inside this cluttered icon, but brand new white Nikes are out. Too flashy. Hardware stores are steady, and steady is not flashy. New boots are okay. They will usually elicit some comment, something like, "Dang! New boots . . . price of hogs must be good!"

Men don't shop. They go to the store to get what they already know they want before they go into the store. But a hardware store tempts a man to shop. It is full of great STUFF. None of it is advertised. They hardly ever show a clevis hook on the home shopping channel. And I'm glad. The shopping channel is commercialism; the hardware store is Americana. Give me Americana eight days a week.

Hardware store stuff is stuff you have to have. Or stuff you may need. Same thing. You may already have the item but, someday, you will probably need a different sized one. So you get another one.

You walk the aisles. Tools are everywhere: power tools, fasteners, tool belts, levels, nails, drills and drill bits, routers and router bits, welders, generators, sockets, table saws, power pulls, disk belt sanders, tape measures, grinders, planers, and joiners. And stuff that is variable speed and reversible. And suspenders, the heavy duty kind that come in yellow, red, blue, or black. No mauve. And stuff in dusty boxes stacked on dusty shelves. You look in the boxes. You never know where treasure lurks. And stuff you don't know what is but aren't about to admit you don't know what is. Then there is the stuff that you do know what is, but really don't need at the moment. You love knowing that if you do need it you know where to go to get it. Sometimes you get it anyway because there just is nothing better than being able to say, after something breaks, "Hey, I got one of those. I can fix that." That is a man thing and that is good. That is real good.

Some things in a hardware store are almost sacred, such as circular saws and compressors, wrenches and screwdrivers, and hammers. Take circular saws and compressors. You have to have good ones with power. The reason is, you never want to have to do anything to them. You just use them. Over and over. Toss 'em, drop 'em, run over 'em, they have to keep working or they ain't worth diddly. And if they ain't worth diddly, their brand name is the subject of much ridicule during conversation over the lunch box at noon. In that case, you had better not have one in the back of your pickup truck where people might see it or they'll say, "Geez, where did you get that piece of crap?" For that reason, just find good power tools in real hardware stores.

You can't have too many wrenches and screwdrivers. You just can't. No way. So real hardware stores have lots of them in all sizes and shapes. Because having the right tool for the job is not only necessary, but good. Using a crescent wrench when you need a distributor wrench is not cool.

Take hammers. Your favorite one is prominently displayed over your work bench. It is the one with the wooden handle (that you've replaced at least four times) with the worn black head. It was your first. You don't throw your first hammer away. You use the one with the rubber covered, unbreakable steel handle when you don't want to risk the ol' wooden handled favorite. For all the above considerations, real hardware stores stock lots and lots of hammers, especially the wooden handle variety.

You can't stay any longer because you have work to do. You wouldn't need the tools and stuff if you didn't have a project, so you have to get with it. But the hardware store experience has been good. It always is.

You go to the counter. You don't 'check out.' You put your framitzes on the counter and banter with the proprietor. Not CEO, proprietor. And you get a receipt that has handwriting on it. It says, "FRAMITZ $12—" (no 95's or 85's, just $12—), and it has the proprietor's initials on it.

As you walk out, the screen door closes behind you with a mild slam as you say, "See ya later, Chuck." Chuck says, "Take it easy. Hurry back." And he actually means it.

Out in the truck, the receipt goes on the dashboard with all the rest of the ones from previous visits for the last five years. The framitz goes on the seat beside you or, if it's a big framitz, in the bed of the truck. As you drive off, you feel good because you just had the pleasure of visiting a vanishing breed, the real hardware store. You are off to your project with the right tools and the right stuff. Long live the hardware store.

3
ROADSIDE CAFE BREAKFAST

The roadside cafe. The road can't be more than two lanes. Mandatory. More lanes than that and you risk eating the food of big business. You know the kind, where they put pictures of food on the menu. Hey, I didn't come in here for no still life. I want food that speaks for itself.

Here's what to listen for: Pull off the two lane road and hear the sound of gravel in the dirt parking lot. There are no parking lines, you just sort of park where the puddles aren't. The people inside will be looking outside, to see who the heck's coming in. They already know your truck. (If you washed it, you're in for some crap.) You wipe your feet . . . real men wipe their feet when they come from a muddy lot into their favorite breakfast cafe. The door creaks . . . loud . . . and might even have a little bell hanging on it that rattles more than it rings when you jostle it. Everyone looks up. They would look up anyway, even without the noise. They saw you coming when you pulled in, remember? If they don't know you they'll just nod, maybe even say, "Howdy." Then they'll go back to their plates and conversation, keeping an occasional eye on you. If they know you, you are greeted friendly, "Look what the cat dragged in." Or, "Got kicked out of the house again, huh?" Or, "When did they let you out of jail?" The more politically astute might say, "Hell, I thought the government made a bureaucrat out of you and you were hiding and waiting for your retirement check." You can do one of two things, smile and sit down with a casual wave or hurl some insult back. Usually the former is better. You'll get your turn for the latter on the next customer.

That's what a roadside cafe sounds like. You can't get those sounds at one of those picture food places. And remember, if it sits beside a road that has more than two lanes, don't go there. It is not the real thing.

On to the dining experience. Table is Formica with or without some sort of pattern on it. Who the heck cares if there is a pattern on it? It has one chrome leg in the middle to stand on. Benches are covered in naugahyde of some color. Who the heck cares what color it is? Booths are for buddies. The stools at the counter are for when you are by yourself. Doesn't matter a lot. You can converse cross-cafe if you have a good insult you need to heave at someone.

The waitress comes up and says, "Coffee." It's a question, but it doesn't sound like it. You answer it like it is, "You bet." Or even, sometimes, "Please." She is gone, taking the wet towel she used to wipe off the table. You like her. She's working for a living, like you, and working hard. The coffee comes. Thick, porcelain cups with big handles you can get your fingers through. You know it is a real cafe because the waitress is wearing a sweat shirt with the cafe logo on it. And you know the 4X4 parked out back is hers.

The waitress pulls a small white pad from her back jeans pocket and a pen from behind her ear, folds back a few pages of the pad, holds it in front of her in the palm of her left hand, poises the pen over it with her right hand and then looks at you. Just looks at you. Some may say, "What'll it be?" or "What can I get ya?" But it is not a requirement. It is time to order. You have to order big. Eggs and bacon and sausage and hash browns and hotcakes and stuff. You do. She writes it down, something like 2 OE SAUS or SCRAM BAC. She leaves and clips the order on a round thing hanging over the area separating the kitchen from the counter and hollers, "Order!" She hollers it loud, too. That is another sound of a real breakfast cafe.

The food comes in a deep oval platter, so you can push it around and stab it and keep eating while you are carrying on an important fishing conversation at the same time. The eating is almost incidental. Sure, it fills you up for a day of fishin' or equipment operating or hammering, but the real enjoyment was the experience—great insults, good lies, belly laughter, and no nonsense food and service. Before you leave you enter the drawing for a free fishing pole. On your way out you hear, "Stay out of trouble" and "Don't let the door hit you in the butt on the way out." And that same creaky, squeaky ol' door says in its own way, "Y'all come back now, ya hear?"

You just had breakfast with the boys at a roadside cafe. It's a great way to start the day.

4
TRACTORS

Tractors are generally man things. They are awesome. They are so powerful, so purposeful. You just love to run them. You sit up high, cradled with a steering wheel . . . and levers and pedals and buttons and toggles and power. You can see far, see dirt and mud and things that you can do. And on a tractor you can do them: move stuff, scrape, plow, plant, cultivate, push, pull, dig, mow, haul, carry, furrow, harvest, or just drive around in a big field on a warm day and look at the livestock. Or you can sit on the ground resting your back on one of the big rear tires and eat your lunch and gaze out at all the plowing you did that morning.

Tractors come in all sorts of sizes and shapes and colors, from large to small, from green, blue, red, and orange, to rust. It really doesn't matter, as long as it's a tractor. An old tractor, with rust here and there, a seat with the paint worn off, that has been earning a living for thirty years, and is still earning a living, is about as perfect a thing as there is on this earth. It is old, but it runs *oh* so smooth and does what it does well. Man, it makes you feel good just being there and sharing life with it. This tractor is forever and when you are on it you are forever, too. And the huge new tractors that pull an eight-bottom plow . . . wow! You just a-sittin' up there, one with the land, helping it produce. You are doing something, *really* doing something. And you can see the result of your work. Just look behind you and see all that rich soil being turned over and layered anew for nature to spawn its miracles. You can smell the soil and the power of the diesel. And you can feel the steady, rhythmic vibrations of the soul of the machine, working, pulling, working, working, working. And you are there on the tractor. Oh, it's good; it's *soooo* good.

Take a Caterpillar type tractor, it is different but just as awesome. When you are on one of those you are where you want to be. You are really purposeful. You can't go on the asphalt or concrete of civilization. You are one with where you are. They are not fast and it doesn't matter, because they are so darn strong. They can push and pull like no other and you are their master, all nestled in the seat with great levers to operate and the thing does what you tell it to do. And you sit there with those tracks on either side of you, going around and around, kicking up dirt and dust, just doing their thing. No whining. No excuses. Just purpose. Doing stuff that matters. Yeah, cat-tractors make you feel good.

Tractors are dirty and that is good. You drive one and you come home dirty, dirt and dust everywhere, caked into every crevice of your clothes. When you come home after a day of tractor driving, you don't just feel like you've done something, you *look* like you've done something. You are lookin' good, *real* good. And your ball cap with the tractor logo and sweat stains on it has dust all over it, too. You can knock the dust off your cap by slapping it on your knee, but that's it. You can wash the clothes, but not the tractor ball cap. Never. Because when you have a dirty tractor-logo ball cap on while you're down at the feed store, you are *somebody*.

Then there is hangin' around people who like old tractors. They *like* things. It is fun being around people who like things. When you are around people who like things, they are less likely to bitch about things. Tractor people like things.

In a perfect world every man would have some land and a tractor. There would be a pile of dirt at one end of the land. In the morning, the man would go out and use the tractor front loader and pick up the dirt one scoop at a time and move it to the other end of the property. The next day he would move it back. Or he could just plow. Plow one way one day and another way the next day. That would be livin'. That would be a man thing.

I've often said to my wife—she usually just smiles back at me and nods—that I'd like to start a business called "Plowers Anonymous." It would be on a big plot of ground and men would come and rent a tractor and plow, or scoop, or dig, stuff like that. Hey, if I built it, they would come! Promise. Women would be allowed but it would mostly be men that came. Playing in the dirt is mostly a man thing. We could even have meetings.

Writing this has me all excited. If you buy enough of this book, I'm going to get another tractor. I think I'll drive it to work and the grocery store. Tractors are very acceptable, very in. They are not in *Vogue* or *Gentlemen's Quarterly*, but that's because it is understood they are cool. When you are on a tractor, you are not pretending to be anybody. You are just who you are and you are comfortable with that. Yeah, another tractor. A man can't have too many tractors.

5
TOOL BELTS

The tool belt is one of the greatest adornments a man can wear. Yeah, it is a man thing. I have never seen a fashion model wear a tool belt at one of those New York or Paris shows.

The tool belt is thick and strong. It can make a waist out of almost any belly. It has holsters and holders and pouches and clips and snaps and loops. There are all sorts of places to hang and put stuff. There are places to put enough tools to fix the world. The hammer dangles from its holder, at the ready to fix the architectural wrongs of any house; the drop-jaw pliers in their holster, poised to reduce plumbing nightmares to pleasant dreams; the pouch full of wire nuts, waiting to repair any electrical glitch that any full moon might bring. All of this surrounded by a bevy of screw drivers, long, short, flathead and Phillips, to tighten or loosen whatever they must, and framed by twenty-seven hundred wrenches and one ubiquitous tape measure. Then, just to top it off, the tool belt pouch collection is garnished with an assortment of nails and screws, wood, metal, galvanized, box, and common. With your tool belt, you are saddled up and prepared for man work. You are Jesse James and the Lone Ranger at the domestic ready. When you wear it, you are so powerful, so-o-o capable, s-o-o ready. Gawd, I love a tool belt. . . .

The best tool belts are made of leather. Genuine leather. *Thick* genuine leather. New ones are okay, but older is best. It means you have been a successful fixit-man longer. An inherited one is an heirloom, a silent monument to things fixed past.

When you put your tool belt on, you get that faraway look in your eye. THAT look. The look that says, "Look out things. You are about to be fixed." You walk around the house a lot with your tool belt. Broken things cringe. Too, there is something about the way a tool belt hangs. At an angle. A bit cocky. And there is something about its weight. It makes you walk with a bit of a swagger. Yeah, it is the angle and the weight that make you walk that way.

Proper tool belt usage dictates that whenever you walk up to what needs to be fixed, you reach for the proper tool without ever taking your eyes off what you are fixing. Then, when you are done with the first tool, you put it back and pull out the next tool, again without looking. It is so cool to do that. Your tool belt is a part of you. It's like you don't have to look at your head to scratch it. (Head scratching is seldom allowed anyway; it implies doubt and doubt is not a man thing.)

The worst thing about a tool belt is having to take it off. When you do, it exposes your mortality. You become a house surgeon without a scalpel, a mere mortal. So it is important that you place it in an obvious and ready place of honor. Ready for your next swaggering foray into fixit land. . . .

The tool belt is armor for the soul.

6
CAMPFIRE BISCUITS

This isn't about just any biscuits, but campfire biscuits.

Early in the morning at the campsite, you wake up from a warm and dry night in your sleeping bag. The morning is clear and crisp. Your camping partner has already built the fire. It is crackling, nestled in a circle of large river rocks. You can see a little smoke and a few ashes rising and falling here and there. You contemplate the setting, and then anticipate breakfast in the mountains. The coffee pot is already by the fire. You look forward to topping it off with some "man biscuits."

"Man Biscuits:" Bisquick and water, ball it up in a tin bowl, pull off little pieces, roll and flatten, put them on a tin plate and put the plate on the fire. Drink another cup of coffee, feel the fire, and take in the morning. It is clean, cool, fresh, and free. You don't have to say much. You just feel a lot. You feel a lot that is good. The biscuits are cooking; they'll be ready when they're ready.

You are dressed appropriately for the dining, good boots, dirty blue jeans that conform to your body because you've been wearing them for two weeks, plaid flannel shirt, unbuttoned down vest and a ball cap with jagged sweat stains above the bill. If Emily Post had a clue about real life, she would be proud.

Hey, the biscuits look about ready. They are rising. One side is brown to burned and the other side is mushy. And they are garnished with a few ashes. Kick the plate away from the fire with your foot, use a leather glove to pick up the plate, and set it on the stump by the coffee cups. A couple of biscuits slide off the plate and land on the ground. No sweat. Pick them up and blow them off. Stubborn dirt can be removed by flicking it with your finger. These biscuits will be eaten first. It's the man thing to do.

Grab one and break it open. A little steam rises and it is almost cooked clean through. It doesn't matter if it isn't. You made it and it is man food. You wash it down with a swallow of coffee. Your partner says, "Man, these biscuits ain't for shit." That is a compliment. If he didn't like them, he wouldn't say anything. Man etiquette. He grabs two more with one hand. Eat the next one with a little honey. Get honey on your hand and wipe it on your pants. Now we are talking gourmet. It just doesn't get any better than this.

Save some for later. A little biscuit and peanut butter at noon will go well while sitting behind the fishing pole. It is something else to look forward to.

You made them. You ate them. You washed them down and their internal expansion is satiating. Doing the breakfast dishes is actually nothing more than a scraping. Actually, you didn't give the experience—and that's what it was, an experience—much thought. It was just breakfast on the mountain. The morning just sort of wrapped around those biscuits. They were simple and good. And they set the tone for a darn good day.

7
ASKING FOR DIRECTIONS

Directions? Men don't ask for them. Men don't need to. They have the sun, the moon, the stars, the wind, landmarks and the coreolus. (Even if they don't know what the coreolus is, they still have it.) Not to mention the flow of the river, the direction of the breeze and an innate, powerful sense of direction. Ask for directions? No way. That would be wimpy. Or wussie. Not to mention uncharacteristic and, well, defeatist. Ask for directions? Nope. I will find it; I will figure it out.

"It's right over here somewhere. I'll just work my way to it, a couple lefts, a couple rights, and I'll see something I recognize. No, I don't need the map. I know about where it is; I was around here ten years ago. I'll find it, okay?!!?!?! See, I think we're getting close.

"Yes, I see the gas station. Ask that guy? You gotta be kiddin'. Look at him. He's a jerk. He doesn't know where he is, let alone where I have to go. I am not asking him, no way. I said I would figure it out. We are getting close; I know it. So what if we're a little late. We'll get there. I know what I'm doing. You are NOT getting out of the car. I might not be able to find you. Ha! That was a JOKE! I meant it as a joke, okay? To be funny. I was JUST kidding. It is right off this street. I know it is. No, I am not asking that kid on the corner. He's got his hat on backwards. About all he could tell me is where the nearest video store is, or what channel the *Simpsons* are on.

"Hey, I have found stuff before, haven't I? I haven't been lost my whole life, you know. No, I am NOT lost now. YOU will ask? You don't need to. I've got it figured out. It is right up here. See?!!? No . . . that's not it. But we're close. I can feel it, like Lewis and Clark and Columbus. They knew how to get somewhere. Hell, it is genetic. 'Wrong Way' Corrigan? Nobody is perfect. I may be temporarily disoriented, but I am not lost. North is that way. There are other places around here and I know right where they are. Why did you get so quiet all of a sudden? Cat got your tongue? There it is! See? Yes, it is. Well, maybe not. But that proves we are getting close. I am still going in the right direction. The right direction is the key. As long as you are headed in the right direction, you will get there. There is no way we are lost. They will hold our reservations, money talks. It is not like anyone else in the world has never been late. They held a whole country for Columbus while he was finding his way. I am not Columbus? Cute. Maybe not, but I am finding my way.

"Hey! There it is! I think I found it. Look! That is it. See? I told you. I told you I would find it. Follow your nose. I always find things. I found you, didn't I? I didn't even have to ask for directions."

8
MAN SHOPPING

———————

Determine need, i.e., a hammer.

Drive to hardware store.

Go directly to hammer section.

Get hammer.

Check out.

Drive home.

Turn on football game.

9
FISHIN'

Not fish-ing. Men don't go fish-ing. They go fishin'.

A fishin' trip to your favorite lake with one of your good buddies goes something like this: You are up early, the whole family is still asleep. They know Dad has had this trip planned for three weeks. It is his day.

You make a quick lunch of a couple PB & J's and a baloney on white bread, wrap them up and throw them in a paper bag. You fill up the old faded and beat-up green thermos with coffee. It has been drop-kicked, run over, and used as a football. Your thermos is old faithful. When it is with you all is secure, all is well. You grab the box of donuts and head out the door to hook the boat to the truck. Outside it is dark and cool. There is just a hint of an orange glow on the horizon, the precursor to a grand day on the lake.

Your buddy arrives in your driveway dressed like you: faded blue jeans, plaid shirt, vest, and filthy ball cap. He throws his thermos in your truck and helps you hook up the boat. You don't have to say much at this point; you know what has to be done and you just want to get there and get out on the water. You both hook up the boat by lifting and dragging the trailer over to your truck and coupling it to the hitch. The boat is an old faithful: aluminum, used, full of character, and hosed off once a year whether it needs it or not. It reeks of good times. There are a few things a man can count on in this life. His wife, his dog, his thermos, and his boat are right up there at the top of those things.

You pull out of the driveway and head for the lake. It is still dark. Dark is good at this point. It means you will be arriving at the lake just before dawn.

On the road you pull out the donuts and coffee. The guy not driving pours. That first cup of coffee in the morning while heading to the lake for a day of fishin' is almost a religious experience. No! It IS a religious experience. You talk with your mouth full of donuts about how Al said they were biting on flies last week at the north end of the lake. Darin just went yesterday and caught some closer to shore with worms. Fishin' talk. You are either going to catch some or not, and you are going to try a little bit of everything to do it no matter what anybody says. But you still have to talk about what Al and Darin did. It is just what you do when you go fishin'.

At the lake you wheel around and back the boat to the launch. Your partner unloads and holds it while you pull the truck and trailer out of the way. You grab the rest of the donuts, the lunch, thermos, poles and tackle boxes and trundle down to the boat. You toss the stuff in and then you both climb aboard and push off . . . and you are THERE AT LAST . . . floating . . . and the world slows down, way down. No motors on this lake, you float and row or paddle. That's the way it is.

You drift out, mist rising lazily off the lake, just the sound of oars going into the water and water dripping off the oars as they come out of the water. All is peaceful, all is slow. World problems do not exist, politics don't happen, and neither fame nor money are more important or better than what you are doing at this very moment. You are floating, serene, at peace, and happy. You are fishin'.

You pour another cup of coffee and wedge the cup with your foot in the bottom of the boat while you get your pole ready. You toss your first line out about the same time the first ray of sunshine streaks over the mountain tops and strikes a shimmering golden hue upon the lake's ripples. The line sits, you sit, and you sip your coffee. You admit to yourself that the fish are not the only reason you are here. You are here just to be here.

Occasionally, from across the lake, you hear the muted sounds of a few other fishermen in their boats, talkin' and rowin' and floatin' and fishin'. If you come within 'recognition range' of any of them, you just nod in their direction. They are content in their natural solitude.

Sometimes you even catch something. You feel the tug and wiggle on your line as you consummate the hunt for food as mankind has done from time immemorial. You pull and reel and do battle to obtain nourishment to sustain your very survival. It is you alone against the elements. You are locking horns with nature, sensing victory in the struggle, excited, pumped. This is a fish you can bring home for all to see, the conquering hero. You pull the fish in, admire the 8" monster, put it in your creel and pull out your baloney sandwich. Life is good now, uncluttered, understandable, honest, and pure.

Your partner hauls one in, too. You share the excitement of his bounty, discuss the details of the struggle, and enjoy the after-glow of the victory. You both catch two or three, and that is enough. You are not greedy, but you are good enough to be able to catch food.

You drift some more, satiated. The hunt complete, you can now take in the purity of the morning. The water is glistening, the air is fresh. The gentle sounds of nature are all around you. You savor friendship and the last PB & J. You are not ready to go.

Finally, it is time to go, but you go with the thought that you are going to do this again soon. You head for shore, load up, clean the fish, and head for home.

At home you unload. The family comments on your smell, but they let you show them your fish. They are politely impressed. The fish go into the freezer, to be eaten sometime later. Who cares? You went fishin' and the fishin' was good.

10
PICKUP TRUCKS

Pickup trucks are not just a man thing, but a man necessity. They are a right. They are part of a man's wardrobe. But they have to meet several man standards.

If nothing else, pickup trucks have to be tough. They don't have to be clean or new. They do have to be tough. They have to be such that all you ever do to the darn things is put in gas and sometimes oil. And they better be able to go 250,000 - 300,000 miles without a whimper. And they have to be such that if you drop the Rock of Gibralter in the bed from a height of 250 feet, the truck barely flinches. They have to be big, broad-shouldered, barrel-chested and dirty. Smaller trucks are okay in their place, as long as they have a toughness about them.

Pickup trucks can have advertised features on them, nice little gizmos and stuff, but no carpet on the floor. With rubber floor matting you can just hose the thing out if you need to. Leather seats are out. You're going to work in this thing, not go to the prom. Inside, they have to have tough seats and a good dashboard; tough seats so you can throw all your stuff on them and do no harm and a good dashboard so you can throw a three year accumulation of receipts up there and it barely makes a difference. Tires have to be big with some gnarly tread, mounted on some big ol' honkin' wheels, all framed by a big chrome rear bumper. Now we are getting somewhere. . . .

Some pickup trucks have lights across the top of the cab, but here you have to be careful. Bug deflectors, external windshield visors, etc., are risky. Too much of that plastic foo-foo and you spoil the essence of tough and practical. Leave that ticky-tacky stuff off. You want something that looks good dirty. Foo-foo don't look good dirty. Bed liners are okay, however. You can haul steer manure by day, hose it out, then haul a dozen red roses home to your wife at the end of the day. A tool box across the back of the bed is okay, too. You can throw all your stuff in there and lock it, but still have a bed for hauling.

A couple other things about pickup trucks are man important: noise and mileage. For noise it can't go 'mmmmmmmmmmm.' It has to have a low rumble to it, one that says, "I can pull and climb and haul and work all day, easy." And mileage? Don't talk about it. Working pickup trucks don't get mileage. Period. Sitting up high is important, too. A truck that sits too low is painfully close to being a car. Four-wheel drive and you know you're sittin' in a truck.

Put your truck to use and you are really somebody. Haul a load of hay, a bunch of feed sacks, a stack of fence posts, a stock rack with a couple cows, some shovels and a crow bar, several rolls of barbed wire, stuff like that, and your man status soars. Pull a flatbed trailer with a tractor that has a front loader on it and you are untouchable in man land. I mean, who is going to argue with you? You are goin' somewhere and doin' something. It doesn't get any better than that.

When you are haulin' or pullin', your truck can't look all squatty or have its tail draggin'. If it does, it is not the real thing. The real thing plans for the heavy stuff, with heavy duty springs and shocks. The squatty ones are weekend pretenders.

Pickup trucks are at their best off the main road. Turn off the blacktop and take off across the field, into the mud, through the snow, over hill, over dale, and you have escaped the mundane existence of those trapped on the concrete in their routine, pitiful, small, regular, pukey cars. Pickup trucks in the dirt put you in man land. Aaaaargh!

Pickup trucks *define* man land.

11
BARBER SHOPS

———————

Barber shops are man places. Not "Clip 'n' Curl." Or "Perm 'n' Grease." Or "Dew 'n' Dash." Just barber shop. Usually they are tucked in between some big buildings, or in a corner someplace. Most commonly they are just a small hole in some wall. But it is a hole in the wall that you like to go to. You get your hair cut, but that is just part of it. You go just to go. There's a lot of stuff that goes on in a barber shop, and it's all good stuff.

Real barber shops say BARBER SHOP on the front plate glass window. They say it in big gold letters. They might even say BUD'S BARBER SHOP or FRANK'S BARBER SHOP. No matter whose shop it is, it has to have, yup, you guessed it, a real, live barber pole out front. Red and blue stripes on a white background, going round and round. The barber pole going round and round is saying, "This is the real thing, a barber-shop barber-shop." It is safe to go in. No surprises.

You go in. There are one or two barber chairs, three max, on a linoleum floor. There are piles of different color hair at the bases of the chairs with a big mirror on the wall behind them, along with counters full of clippers and scissors and combs and stuff. The place smells good, too. It's kind of after-shavey. No receptionist up front pulling on her gum and sitting behind a desk with a big appointment book here. Nope. If the barber chairs are full, you just nod and say, "How ya doin'?" Then you sit down in one of the waiting chairs by the wall. The waiting chairs have no motif. Some are plastic, some

41

are wood, and some are whatever. Maybe there is a motif; you could call it 'early barber shop.' It doesn't matter. You aren't in there for *Vanity Fair* stuff.

If you are the only customer in the barber shop, you are next. If you are the third guy, you are number three. It is easy. Those are the rules. Appointments are for doctors not to keep; they are not for real barber shops. If you are so important or busy that you need an appointment, then you are too important and busy. Everybody is equal in a barber shop. That is part of the charm. Need an appointment? Go to "Dew 'n' Dash."

There is always conversation going on in a barber shop. You can just listen or jump right in. Either is acceptable. Barbers are amazing people. One customer can be a Democrat ranting about the Republicans and the next guy can be a Republican lambasting the Democrats, and the barber just smiles and nods. Both customers leave thinking they have been agreed with and liking their barber. Like I said, barbers are amazing people. In reality, political discussions are generally somewhat subdued. You don't go to a barber shop for controversy; there is enough of that outside the shop. There is more talk of fishin' and sports and the weather than anything else. And passion and opinions abound on those subjects, but it is good passion and friendly opinions. It's man talk.

The magazines found lying around are part of the ambiance, and are indicative of the clientele. There are a few news magazines from three or four years ago, but mostly *Field and Stream* and *Sports Afield* and *Sports Illustrated* and *Illustrated Sports* and *Fishin' Digest* and *Truck Trader* and *Man Land* and *Fly Fishin'* and a well worn copy of *Man Things,* not to mention the daily newspaper all folded back and piled in no particular order, but with the sports section always missing. There are no magazines about bric-a-brac or potpourri. You get to pick from a really fine selection of reading material in a barber shop. You either read or talk while you are waiting. A really practiced barber shop customer can do both at the same time.

Usually you just know first names in a barber shop. But they are always good names: Bud and Doyle and Terry and Frank and

Fred and John. Not Fontaine or LaDuke. They are names like a friend would have, and your barber is your friend.

Your turn comes and you climb in the chair and all the familiar stuff happens, the cape, the chair adjustment, and the, "How ya been?" You don't have to tell him how you want your hair cut. He knows. You have been in there lots of times before. He can also pick up the conversation where you left it off three weeks ago, "How'd that roofing project go?" I don't know how barbers can do that. The haircut just sort of happens: clippers buzzing, scissors clipping, and your neck being shaved with lather and a straight razor. Real stuff.

I wouldn't mind being a barber. Good conversations, good magazines, good ol' boys. I just wouldn't want to cut hair. I don't think I would be very good at it. But I can go there and take it all in and participate and even get a darn good haircut in the process.

Barber shops are great places.

12
BUILDING A FENCE

Building a fence puts you in a man zone. You are marking your territory. You are constructing and working and establishing and building a monument all at the same time. It doesn't matter if it is barbed wire around your eighteen-hundred acre cattle ranch, or picket, or lattice, or split-rail, or one-by-six dog-eared cedar around your back yard, it is the same thing. You have to gather your stuff, your tools and materials, and design and build it. And it is great fun.

Take your back yard. You go there and survey your territory, imagine how you are going to mark it, and come up with a plan. Then you get your tools: tool belt, hammer, nails, tape measure, level, shovel, crow bar, stakes, and string. You haul them out back and plop them down, hitch up your tool belt, and you are good to go.

The air is warm, but not hot. The garden hose is nearby if you get thirsty. That is your watering hole. It is where you can drink from the hose and let it run down your chin and watch it splash all over your boots and you don't care. You don't swallow the last mouthful because you are going to swish and spit it out and wipe your mouth with your forearm. You are really cool when you do that.

The spring soil is moist, but not wet, from the winter rains. It will be sweet smelling and good digging. And you have your working ball cap on—the dirty one—as opposed to your go-to-town ball cap. You are primed.

You stake your corners and stretch string between them to mark a straight line. A fence has to be straight. You have to be able to stand at one corner, squint one eye, and see it straight as a rod. That is the sign of a good fence. Since everyone in the Northern Hemisphere worth his salt is going to look down your fence and check it for 'straight,' you must do the job right. From the corners you mark off eight foot centers for your line posts. You are ready to dig.

Digging is good with the shovel and crowbar. Dig down and extract the dirt and pile it into a mound. Admire the soil and the hole. You are one with nature. You start to sweat. Sweat is good. You know you will probably be sore tomorrow, but you are dang sure not going to admit it. You will just move a little slower and hope no one notices.

The holes are dug. Now you get to set the posts, which are the first visible signs of progress and indicators of your planning. Today you are putting eight foot, four-by-four cedar posts in two and one-half feet deep holes. They have to be straight and solid. You put the post in and tamp a little dirt around the bottom to hold it. Then you level it up on all sides with the level. Posts must not only be straight in the line, but not leaning in any other weird direction either. You pour in a little Redi-mix concrete to ensure strength. Strength is important. A fallen fence is a man's ego crushed. The posts are set and you walk to one end and sight down the line. They are straight! You look to the heavens and let out a primal scream. If the neighbors are home, you do this in your mind. You walk up to a couple of the posts, grab them and give them a wiggle. They don't wiggle. They are solid. Another primal scream. You look around to see if anyone is watching. If no one is, you give the posts a couple of hard slaps, sort of a left-right-left combination. They are still solid. Another scream. Now it is time for another quick swig and spit from the garden hose, all the while catching several disguised glimpses of your work and feeling good about it. You are really in man zone now. . . .

It is time for the stringers. Nail them up, right between the posts. Because you measured and dug well, they fit. Well, you had to cut a couple of them, but that was probably the mill's fault. The mill cut them too long. You nail them up solid. Solid is important, remember? Just like straight. Now you get to grab hold of the top stringer and swing from it (if no one is watching). Swing from it. Hang on it. It is a man test. It holds you. Of course it holds you; you built it, didn't you? It is time for another swing and another scream. It is also time to stand back and blatantly admire your work. Not too blatantly. You can stick one hand in your pocket and sort of rub your chin with the other hand, in a thinking and pondering sort of way, like you are in deep man-construction-thought. But what you are really doing is admiring. It is a thin disguise but, dangit, admiring your work is a fringe benefit. You can't be denied a fringe benefit. It wouldn't be right.

Now is a good time for eating the sandwiches you made. Take a quick break. Quick because you don't want to lose your man zone. So you take a position sitting in the dirt and resting your back against a post. You push your ball cap back on your head and take a deep breath of fresh air and eat and admire and admire a little more. Your hands are dirty so the white bread gets hand prints on it but, hell, who cares? It is just a little dirt and a little dirt isn't bad. It is part of the ambiance.

It is time for the nailing of the fence boards. This is the *coup de gras*, the putting up of the one-by-six-by-six dog eared cedar. It is beautiful stuff, hues of pink and light and dark wood colors with some knots thrown in for character. It smells good, too. It would make a great cologne, 'Essence of Cedar.' I don't know where you would wear it. Maybe to the hardware store. The nailing is almost gentle, and it is done with great precision. It is the *au jus*, the whipped cream on the pumpkin pie, the ice cream on the hot apple pie. It is ceremonial. All of the planning and sweat, the straight and the solid is now decorated with the beauty of the cedar fence boards. It is a man thing. They are put up, oh, so straight across the top. This is not hard work. It is the frosting on the cake, to be done with great joy. You don't scream this time. You just stand back and look and smile a tight smile while your chest fills with pride. . . .

Now it is on to the gates. Here we are talking about real planning and precision. We are talking about fit and swing and latching and no sag. You get the drift. I will leave the details to your imagination. Have a good time in man land.

47

13
RULES ABOUT WOMEN

By rules, I mean lessons learned. Over the years. Most of them the hard way. I pass them on here to perhaps save you some pain. I say "perhaps" because no way these rules are complete or even concrete. Women reserve the right to change their minds at any time, but I have sanitized and fool-proofed them as best I can.

When your wife says, "Don't get me anything for my birthday," that does not mean to not get her anything for her birthday.

* * *

When your wife asks you if you want to go shopping with her, she doesn't want you to go shopping with her. She just wants to know that you want to go shopping with her.

* * *

When your wife says, "Look at all the money I saved at the sale," she just spent a lot of money at the sale.

* * *

Never say, "Are you wearing that?" (This may very well be the #1 rule of all the rules.)

Empty the dishwasher without being asked.

* * *

If she walks up to you and says, "Well?" Say, "You look nice." This covers hair, dresses, new earrings, and/or new shoes.

* * *

If she asks, "What's our song?", sing it out loud and clear. If you can't remember it, get laryngitis fast.

* * *

Don't say, "That's really nice. When did you get that?" She got it three years ago and has worn it twenty-seven times and you were there for every one of them.

* * *

Do the laundry without being asked. Recognize, however, that this is always somewhat risky. Sweaters shrink, colors fade, nylons cling, bath towels lint, and shop towels in a washing machine will ruin anything that comes within one light year of them.

* * *

At supper time never say, "What did you put in this?"

* * *

Always eat the sandwich she made you for lunch.

* * *

Never use all the hot water just before she showers.

* * *

Be able to say, "I'm sorry." And mean it.

* * *

When you go to a social event with her, stay with her.

When she's doing a man thing with you, never make fun. Appreciate it.

* * *

If she wants to drive your tractor, let her drive your tractor.

* * *

Tell her how pretty the flowers are that she planted.

* * *

Know the names of some of the flowers she planted.

* * *

Valentine's Day is big, okay? No, it's HUGE. It's a woman thing. Plan and spend accordingly.

* * *

Never assume anything about a woman.

* * *

If nothing else, earn and keep her trust.

* * *

Dress like you care about what she thinks about how you dress.

* * *

Recognize that there is no limit to the number of lessons that can be learned.

* * *

Be there.

* * *

Call home when you are away.

Invite her fishin'. She probably won't go, but she likes to be invited.

* * *

Appreciate pregnancy and childbirth.

* * *

At dinner out, never look at her plate and say, "Man, you must have been hungry!"

* * *

Do tell her, "You're prettier than a brand new saddle." By the time she figures out that's a really great compliment, it'll sink in that you really like her and she'll like it a lot.

* * *

Do not ever abandon that which you helped spawn. That is unmanly to the max.

* * *

When her girlfriends are visiting and you hear them saying, "Men are only good for vehicle maintenance and yard care," it's a good time to go do vehicle maintenance and yard care.

* * *

Buy her a white, mid-length, terry cloth robe with hearts on it. It feels good on her and it's easy to get off her.

* * *

If she made it, wear it.

* * *

Hug. Hug a lot.

* * *

Compliment her in front of other people.

If she disciplined the kids, back her up.

* * *

When she gives a dinner party, help serve and help clean up.

* * *

Never stop telling her you love her. And never stop showing her you love her.

* * *

If she asks, "Which shoes?" or "Which Dress?" say, "You look good in anything."

* * *

When it is your turn to cook, do not put carrots in the meat loaf. If you do, you will hear about it for the next hundred years.

* * *

Notice the new hair-do.

* * *

Sure thing gifts: lingerie, flowers, and, of course, diamonds.

* * *

Notice the new flower arrangement or wall hanging.

* * *

Send flowers just as a random act of random-ness.

* * *

Encourage her in all endeavors.

* * *

If you buy her clothes, better too small than too big.

If you make a mess in the kitchen, clean it up.

* * *

Take the giblets out of the turkey before you put it in the oven. Or you'll hear about that for a few years, too.

* * *

When she just needs you to listen, listen.

* * *

Treat her like you treated her when you were dating. No, treat her even better.

* * *

Love her and you will be loved.

This is just a general sampling. I am sure you have learned some rules of your own. The trick is not only to learn them, but to heed them. A good relationship with a good woman is about as good as it gets. It is a man blessing.

14
MAN BANTER

"Where the hell you been? I've been workin' for an hour already."

"You got here early then."

"It's that piece of crap truck you drive. Broke down, didn't it?"

"I don't think so, Jack. Remember the time I had to tow your truck with mine?"

"No, I don't seem to remember that."

"I'm sure you don't."

"You know what's wrong with your truck? It's got too many syllables."

"Too many what?"

"Too many syllables, you ignorant dweeb. Truck names are supposed to be mono-syllabic."

"Who'd you have for English? Mrs. Campbell?"

"At least I had someone other than a comic book."

"Yeah, right! You sat next to Linda Sue Cochran. That's the only way you got through class."

"Hey, hand me that level over there."

"How's about you get it yourself?"

"How's about I come down off this ladder and get it myself and then beat the hell out of you with it?"

"How's about I bring it to you and crease your butt with it?"

"That'd be nice. Just bring it over here, will ya?"

"Dang! I gotta do my job and yours too."

"Hey, what did you think of that game the other night?"

"Dang refs had their heads up their butts, that's for sure."

"Yeah, they always do. I thought that Searcy kid played a hell of a game, ran right over the top of that kid from South, what's his name? Welke or Wolke or Wookie, something like that."

"Searcy probably has Mrs. Campbell for English. That's why he's so tough."

"You're a real clear thinker, aren't you?"

"At least I can think, butt munch."

"Then why'd you cut that two-by-six six inches too long?"

"It's the saw's fault."

"Right! It's just like the time we were cycle riding and you thought you could make it up that hill and both you and the bike came right back down, separately. Boy, you had a real case of the dumb-ass that day."

"Yeah, like you never fell off a bike. Hell, your Momma never let you ride a two-wheeler until your senior year of high school. Come to think of it, you still have training wheels on that pickup truck of yours, don't you? That's why you were late. You had a training wheel flat."

"At least I can cut a two-by-six the right length."

"It was the tape measure's fault."

"Next thing you're gonna say is that it was the board's fault."

"It was."

"You know what your problem is? You gotta be smarter than the board, and you're not."

"I'm smart enough to kick your ass."

"Yeah, you and five other guys, maybe."

"Hey, why'd you throw that caulking on the ground? It's bad for the ecology."

"I'll give you ecology. What you want me to do with it? Eat it? Tell you what, I'll feed it to you for lunch."

"Is the boss coming by today?"

"How the hell should I know? Am I clairvoyant or something?"

"If you don't stop using those big words, we're going to have to make a bureaucrat out of you. That way, you can just sit around and do nothing and use big words."

"Whoa! Politics one-oh-one. Who pulled your chain?"

"That dog-breath inspector came around yesterday. We had to re-pour some of the footing. It was an inch off."

"Tell you what, next time he comes around, let's take his little badge and his car keys and sort of accidentally drop them in the cement while we're pouring it."

"You're one smart sumbitch, you know that?"

"That's what everyone tells me."

"Yeah, right after they tell you how ugly you are."

"Hey, you wanna go have a beer after work?"

"So I can buy again?"

"Hell, you ain't bought since the sun rose in the West."

"Bull! I bought the last time you sawed a board wrong, and that happens almost daily."

"Okay, I'll buy. You wanna go or not? I need someone to protect me from all the women who think I'm so cool."

"Yeah, sure. Won't be hard to protect you. That woman who told you you were cool won't be there. She's in reality therapy right now. By the way, do you have any idea what they are saying when they tell you, 'Get a life?'"

"I think they're telling me I'm the coolest dude they've ever seen."

"Yeah, I think that's it."

"I'm just gonna have one beer, though. Molly's making lasagna tonight."

"You're lucky you've got a good woman. I don't know what she sees in you though."

"Yeah, I'm lucky. It's been a darn nice break from hangin' around with a pud-knocker like you. You wanna go fishin' Saturday? Molly's got some deal at the Y in the morning."

"Yeah. Let's go up the Santiam. I hear they're biting up there."

"Done deal. Be at the house at five. And don't be late, or I'll leave your ass."

"No sweat. I got a real truck, remember?"

"Kiss my butt."

Know that at no time during this conversation were any feelings hurt. It was just normal, everyday, run-of-the-mill, man banter. And now these two guys have to go out into the world and be sensitive. It is not easy being a man.

15
PRIVATE PLACES

"WARNING: What you are about to read may be harmful to your psyche. It contains adult situations and adult language. It also contains stuff you didn't even know you didn't want to know. It is, well . . . ah . . . shall we say . . . indelicate. But it is the truth, the whole truth, and nothing but the truth. Only those who have been potty trained will be allowed to read beyond this paragraph, for it is only they who will understand."

Urinals. They are what line the wall in what we call the "men's room." You are about to experience what goes on in there. Be strong. Men go there, literally, but it is not where they are at their best, okay?

There are a lot of different techniques displayed during urinal usage. The conventional methodology is to unzip, go, zip, flush, wash hands, and leave. We wish it was always that simple. But man is always experimenting, isn't he? He is experimenting with different techniques, fighting boredom, trying to improve on what he does. The urinal is no exception to that fact. There is little you can do to improve on the conventional methodology, but that does not prevent men from trying. There is the hands-on-hips technique, unzip, ready, aim, fire, put hands on hips, look up at the ceiling, and sigh a long sigh. Distance from the urinal must be adjusted as pressure decreases. This is done by shuffling the feet forward as the flow diminishes. Conventional methodology guys will generally take up a position two or three urinals away from the hands-on-hips guys; no hands guys need their space. Then there are the head-resters. They unzip and go but during the going they put their forearm on the wall in front of them and lean their head on it. Oftentimes this entire procedure is carried out with their eyes closed. Someone standing next to them might say, "Rough night, huh?" This is generally acknowledged with a weak nod of the head. Head-resters take a long time. Two or three conventional methodology guys may come and go while a head-rester carries out his one task.

There are other techniques, but I think you get the picture. This brief expose is just to wet your interest. You may even have some techniques of your own that you want to pass on. You can do so by writing, "Dear Abby." Additional information on the subject can be found at your local library under "urinals," or on the Internet by clicking the urinal icon. Or by writing http://gotta go.wiz.com.

But we can't leave the discussion just yet. There are other things that go on at urinals. Our quest for the whole truth is not complete until we get them out in the open. It is time to be strong again. Here is what else men do at urinals: They spit. They belch. They sigh. And they break wind. There. It's out. I'm sorry for the shock effect, but at least now that it's out we can begin on the road to healing. Or can we?!!?

Men spit while at urinals. I don't know why, but they do. It is automatic or autonomic or something. Maybe it's Pavlovian. It is not exactly like professional baseball players who, when the camera points at them, spit three times. (Playing a baseball game and then going to a urinal has to be dehydrating.)

They belch. Big ol' loud "baruuups." And they just keep looking straight ahead after they do it and nobody pays any attention or says anything. It would be poor etiquette to do so.

They sigh. A lot. I think it is relief from the relief. I throw it in here because it is probably the nicest thing men do while at urinals.

It is the least offensive to outside observers.

Breaking wind is tacky and offensive. Yet it is done with great regularity, right there at the urinal. Blaaaat-t-t! Nothing much is said. That would be impolite. The act often inspires a spirited competition. Remember the WARNING? I told you there were things you didn't really want to know.

Okay, there is everything you wanted to know about what goes on at urinals. I have to take yet one more liberty and tell you a story. It is a true story. A young twenty-something lady goes into a restroom. Seeing urinals on the wall she realizes she is in the wrong room. At the same time of her realization, she hears someone coming into the room. She panics and rushes into the nearest stall and jumps up on the commode. A man enters. He is obviously a hands-on-hips guy, and proceeds to give a solo demonstration of every disgusting man trick in the book. Long sighs, "Aaaaaaaugh." (He's probably staring at the ceiling all the while.) Then he gargles and spits, follows it with a belch and tops it all off with the "blaaaat" indiscretion. The girl-on-commode is horrified. Nothing in life has prepared her for this. (This book was not yet in print.) In the vernacular she was, ". . . like totally grossed out." The man-animal zips, flushes (at LEAST he flushed), and leaves. The girl-on-commode finally opens her eyes and un-scrinches her face. She is shaken by the ordeal but she is strong, a survivor. Hearing no other noises, she comes down off the commode and makes her escape. Outside, she spots her boyfriend. His back is turned to her. He turns and asks, "Where were you?" Before she could answer, he adds, "I went in the men's room and when I came out you were gone." Had he been an observant man (which, of course, there is no such thing), he would have noticed her eyes open VERY wide as it dawned on her that it was HIM in the rest room. It was all too much for her. She broke up with him the next day.

Urinals are private man places. Believe me, no one else would want to go there.

16
MAN FASHION

Man fashion? There is no such thing. Put your eyebrows back down. What about suits and vests and neckties and Gap and Dockers and polo ponies and all that stuff? Plumage. It is just plumage. To find true man clothes you have to see what men are wearing when they are doing man things. I will give you a couple of hints. In two words: *practical* and *comfortable*. Synonyms would be: cotton and denim. Clean is not necessarily an issue in all this. So let us drop the fashion myth. Let us focus on what men wear in their natural habitat. Let us focus on man clothes.

First, however, we have to visit some of the man philosophy behind man clothes. One, clothes don't matter. They just don't. The focus is on what you are *doing*, not what you are wearing. You put clothes on to do what you have to do. Period. If they work, that is plenty good enough. Two, colors don't matter. You are not going to look at them, just wear them. Three, men don't pay attention to what other men wear. Who cares? Remember, you are dressing for the job of doing man things, not anything else. Remember also, we are talking about men in their natural habitat, not about men playing roles in society and dressing to someone's expectation.

The everyday application of all this is that when men dress they just put clothes on. They don't try them on for looks or color or whatever. They just put them on to put them on. When they open the dresser drawer they wear what is on top. Once they have something comfortable, something favorite, they wear it again. And again. And again. It works and that is all that matters. That is why blue jeans are a favorite. They work. They mold to the body and hold dirt real well. It takes a while to put a good patina on them. When jeans get to where they can stand alone in a corner, then it is usually time to think about washing them. Usually, but not always. Jeans are man's friend, and washing them changes the chemistry. But, contrary to popular belief, odor is not a man thing, so men do wash them. Also contrary to popular opinion, men don't do man work all the time. They go out sometimes, like to have fun. And they generally wash their jeans when they do that. Take the ol' work jeans, wash 'em up, and wear 'em out to the party. It works. Or at least we think it does. Our jeans are part of our psyche, a delicate part of our psyche.

Now let's talk about some man clothes that will really make your heart go pitty-pat: coveralls. Good ol' coveralls. Pull 'em on and you are ready to roll, literally, on the shop floor, under cars, trucks, tractors, whatever. Roll in places only men roll. They get filthy and it doesn't matter. Doesn't matter at all. Get done and take 'em off and your jeans and T-shirt are relatively clean. It is a great concept.

And overalls. Bib overalls. The very fortunate among us have two pair, one blue denim and another gray with blue stripes, railroad type. A work pair and a go to town pair. When you are up on a tractor and wearing bib coveralls, hell, ain't no body gonna mess with ya. There's nothing not to like. You've got it all. And just to illustrate how fortunate I am, I once wore my go-to-town bibs to a friend's house for dinner, with a white shirt and black bow tie. Got invited back, too.

Something else about bib overalls: they can smooth out almost any belly. And there is a place to hang your hammer. You don't see Dockers down at the John Deere store.

Okay, I'll let up. I'm writing this poolside at a Phoenix, Arizona resort. I don't know where you are reading this, but it is not in man land. Men don't read in man land. But at poolside, or wherever you are, just thinking about returning to man land and wearing man clothes kinda gets us all teary eyed, doesn't it? I can't wait to get my bib coveralls on when I get home. Hold on tractor, I'm coming.

The downside of all this—if there is a downside—is that we men sometimes get accused of, well, underdressing. As in, "You're wearing *that*?"

"Well . . . yeah. What's wrong with it?"

"It doesn't match."

"Match what?"

"Anything. The top doesn't match the bottom."

"It doesn't?"

"No. You can't wear plaid with stripes."

"Why not?"

"You just can't"

"I already put 'em on."

"So?"

"When you put something on, you can't take it off. It's on for the duration. It's a man rule."

"Here, let me help you," she says, as she begins unbuttoning my shirt.

"That's all you think about, isn't it? Undressing me."

"Yeah, right," she responds, while at the same time rolling her eyes as she picks out another shirt and lays it on the bed. She calls it a "solid." That must mean all one color, because that's what it is. Then she's off to finish getting dressed herself, having helped you make the transition from man clothes to "fashion." But, you know, other than having to change shirts—very difficult—it's okay.

Occasionally men take fashion into their own hands, with generally predictable results. My friend Dave—he's a magician with a back-hoe—wore some pants to work that had holes in the crotch. Thing was, when he got off work, he and his wife, Stacy, were going to go look at new pickup trucks. Dave called Stacy at noon to see if she would to be ready to go right after work. Stacy asked, "Dave, are you wearing those pants with the holes in the crotch?"

"Yeah. Why?"

"You can't wear those."

"I fixed 'em," Dave said, proudly.

"How?"

"Duct tape."

Stacy, incredulous, "Duct tape?"

"Yeah. You just kinda wrap a couple figure eights around your legs and through the crotch."

"No, Dave."

"No?"

"No."

"Okay."

The change of clothes was worth it. A few hours later, Dave was driving home in a big, new, honkin' 4X4 pickup truck. It was an acceptable trade-off.

As you can see, we come by our propensity for man clothes (or lack of fashion) quite honestly. We can use a little help from time to time. It's like I tell my wife, "I didn't marry you just for your brains and beauty, but to help make me presentable on those occasions when I have to venture outside man land."

17
LOVE

You are probably wondering what this chapter is going to say. So was I, because men don't know squat about love. Or they think they don't. Or they act like they don't. Women know they don't. Actually, men do know about love. They just forget sometimes. It gets obfuscated in man land. But it is there. And they learned it early in life. I know this because I recently read what a third grade class thought love was, and here's what the boys wrote:

"Love is being friendly to others and being respectful to others, too."

* * *

"Love is being adopted and having my dog lick me in the face when I get home."

* * *

"Love is my dog. I want to see him again. He will always be in my life."

* * *

"Love is: The Answer."

"Love is the feeling that you feel for someone or something. It means you care deeply for them."

* * *

"Love is when boys bug girls."

* * *

"I think love is a feeling of passion."

* * *

"Love is when you care for and like someone a whole lot."

* * *

"Love is what parents do at night."

* * *

"Love is kissing and holding hands."

* * *

"Love is how you feel to people and others."

* * *

"Love isn't always just kissing and that other gunk."

* * *

"I think love is when you like someone a lot more than just as a friend."

* * *

"Love is when you get candy hearts on Valentines."

"Love is something between two people."

*   *   *

"Love is Christmas morning."

*   *   *

"Love means to me when someone is caring, such as when someone is hurt, and someone else will go over to them and be caring and say, 'Are you OK?'"

*   *   *

"Love is something you can only feel inside."

*   *   *

"I think love is my feelings in my heart."

See? First we learned love. Then, later, we learned how to be jerks. Once we get past jerk-hood, we come back to love again. It is an awkward cycle. We think we show love when we let her ride in our truck. Or when we let her help build the fence. In our minds, sharing man land is love. Like I said, it isn't easy being a man. Just keep the faith. We will come around.

18
THE CROWBAR

The crowbar? Hey, it was a big part of my life when I was growing up. I was a boy on the farm, but the crowbar introduced me early on to the world of man things. My Mom never had to use the crowbar; she did everything else on the farm, but not the crowbar. I was the crowbar operator; my Dad was the supervisor of the crowbar operator. He didn't believe in slavery, but sometimes I wondered because I dang sure was his crowbar slave. Dig, pry, lift, leverage, whatever it did, I was on the other end of it. I guess it is kind of ironic that I have sort of a soft spot in my heart for crowbars. I don't know what ever happened to the original one we used on the farm, but it is not worn out. Crowbars don't wear out, only their operators do. But I do know I had to have one when I got grown up and on my own. I will tell you about that purchase in a bit. But, first, some history. . . .

What is a crowbar? It is a great big nail. How's that? Yeah, a big ol' six foot long piece of steel with a sharp tip on one end and a flat head on the other. The pointy end is for digging and prying and the flat end is for tamping the dirt you just dug. Very functional. Very purposeful. Unbreakable. Very hard work.

Our crowbar was in a corner of the barn, and it seemed like every time we went in there we—actually, I—had to use it for something or other. It was heavy, but whatever we—actually, I—had to do with it, it did well. You could lift corners of buildings with it while you put a block or boards or rocks or something under there so the chicken house would stand yet another year. You could leverage the front tractor tire off the ground long enough to get some blocks under the axle for a tire change. You could leverage the plow hitch into position on the tractor. You could even pry a stuck tractor out of the mud. You could pry those two boards apart where the wrench fell between the cracks and reach in and get the wrench. You could use it as a pole vault and try and vault the hitchin' rack, or the ditch, or some hay bales. You had to do these latter things when no one was looking. Fun was not a regular part of a crowbar program, work was. You could even use the crowbar to help get a cow back on her feet after calving, just sort of slip it under her side and lean up on it. She usually got the hint. The new calf liked it, too; it lined things up to nurse. And, when you were fourteen years old or so, you could bench press the crowbar while lying in the tall grass, or do arm curls and clean and jerks. You could look at your muscles while you were doing this and you would see the first hint of muscle definition. That would make you do it more; muscle definition is kind of like the difference between boyhood and manhood.

Mostly the crowbar was for digging post holes. Ten thousand million post holes. Three of them were in soft ground, the rest were in granite. Swear. Again, I was the operator, breaking up the ground by raising the crowbar high above my head and slamming it into the dirt. It broke up about one-sixteenth of an inch of ground at a time. That is how it seemed, anyway. My Dad would scoop out the loose dirt, stand back, lean on the shovel, and I would go back to breaking up the ground in the hole. It was always hot and I was always dripping sweat. I would get an occasional peek at the muscles in my forearm and I would think, "Cool, man," and keep diggin'. I'm not sure, but occasionally I think I saw a small, wry smile on my Dad's face while I was operating the crowbar. At least I think that's what it was. I don't know what he was smiling about, 'cause I knew I was a darn sight smarter than he was and there wasn't much funny about being on the ignorant end of that crowbar in the hot sun all day long.

I don't remember getting tired using the crowbar, just impatient. I just wanted to get finished so I could hike the three miles to my friends house and we could go fishin'. Post hole digging cut into that time. I figure from age fourteen to eighteen, I spent fifty percent of my life attached to the crowbar. The side benefit was that we discussed and solved a bunch of the county's problems. Yeah, county's problems. We didn't have world problems back then, didn't have the electronic media bombarding us daily with what was going on bad in Angola and Timbuktu. Even if we had known, wasn't much we could have done about it. And that fact hasn't changed much: Local problems are best handled locally. The crowbar taught me to solve local problems first. The weekly paper told us what was going on and we solved it. If the Sheriff caught the scum bags that stole Martin's saddles, he ought to string the thieving sons-a-guns up by their heels and flog them. Simple. Problem solved.

But there was one problem we never did solve. And we pondered it a lot. I mean a LOT! How come, if you dig the dirt out of a hole and then put a post in the hole, you never had dirt left over after you put the dirt back in the hole around the post? It happened ten thousand million times and we never did figure it out. Figured everything else out, but not that. It remains one of life's mysteries.

Anyway, about my crowbar purchase. I'm grown now, wife, kids, job, house, pets, car, even a television. Everything. Except a crowbar. So, with a few bucks left over, one day I decided it was time. I went to the hardware store (where else?) and walked clean to the back. Crowbars are always in the back, leaning up against the wall. That is what they do when they are not in use. I grabbed one, excited, and hauled it to the front counter. I was second in line. The lady in front of me looked at the crowbar, looked at me, looked back at the crowbar, then looked away, with sort of a quizzical look on her face. The counter help that day was the proprietor's granddaughter. She looked at the crowbar, then looked at me and asked, "What is that?"

"It's a crowbar," I replied.

"What do you do with it?"

Glad to be a part of her educational upbringing, I said, "You dig stuff with it, like holes and ditches. Things like that."

"Oh," was her reply.

Sensing I hadn't made much headway, I added, "It's a man thing."

A wave of recognition came across her face as she tilted her head back and said, "Aaaaaah!"

Then the guy behind me in line chimed in, "Yeah, and I was admiring it, too. It's a fine crowbar."

My Dad's crowbar cost $1.50. Mine cost $23.00. But at least I had arrived; I had a crowbar all my own. My life's pretty much complete now.

The final test was now near: the passing of the crowbar heritage. City kids don't get as much opportunity to dig as we country kids did. With a new house that needed the yard fenced, the opportunity presented itself. My fourteen-year-old son and I gathered up the requisite stuff and headed for the back yard. I got the shovel. He got the crowbar. It was time for transference. One does that by pointing to the ground and saying, "Dig." He did, and it was hot and he sweated and we talked and we solved the problems in Angola and Timbuktu and he looked at his forearms and we lamented the shortage of fill dirt and I smiled. And you know what else? So did he.

The crowbar is not just a man thing. It is a part of the man cycle.

19
GOOD OL' BOYS

What is a good ol' boy? A good ol' boy is sort of a man's man. He is somebody who meets all the requirements for entry into the "Good Ol' Boy Club." Everybody likes him, and that entitles him to be addressed by the hallowed title, "He's a good ol' boy." A genuine good ol' boy is not a jerk or a political animal. He is just a genuine person.

Right off the bat, a good ol' boy is someone you can trust, in business, in card games, with your kids, your wife, your equipment, your tools, your secrets, your dreams. He is someone who is there, who can be counted on. He doesn't judge, gives advice only when asked, is tolerant, and he is someone who does things. No hemmin' and hawin' around, if something needs to be done, he does it. He doesn't wait to be asked, doesn't need to be prodded, just does it.

About equipment (this is an important concept in man land): If a good ol' boy asks to borrow your tractor with the front loader, you loan it to him. You loan it because he would do the same for you. You loan it because you know he will bring it back in a timely manner, in good working order, clean, and full of gas. That is how genuine good ol' boys do things.

And here is something else. If, while he is using your tractor, he falls off the darn thing and hurts himself, he won't sue you or the tractor. He will say, "It was my own dang fault." Lawyers don't get rich off good ol' boys, and that is a blessing, isn't it? What is right has always been better than what lawyers come up with.

Don't think for a minute that a good ol' boy is a wimp. A good ol' boy will take a stand. If something is not right, he will dang sure draw a line in the dirt and stand firm. Early parole for a child molester? Nope. No way. Condemn part of a neighbor's land for a shopping center? That's bull. Sue a car manufacturer because they didn't build a totally indestructible cocoon to protect us from ourselves while driving home drunk? You gotta be kiddin'. That's bunk. Don't back a good ol' boy into a corner. He'll fight for what is right. This country wasn't made great by not standing up for some things that needed to be stood up for.

For the majority of his life a good ol' boy is someone who works hard, puts his family number one, has been married for a long time and wants to stay married for a long time.

He remembers anniversaries and birthdays, sends flowers for no reason, takes his wife out to dinner alone every other week, tells her she looks nice and kisses her every time he leaves the house, and kisses her again when he comes home. He never questions the purchase of the new dress she says she needs. And he is there for his kids, at dinner time, homework time, school play time, sporting events time, prom time, graduation time, and at job and wedding time. At the latter two, he now becomes a friend, offering advice only when asked.

He is also someone who other men come up to and say, "Howdy." And then they shake hands. Good ol' boy handshakes are a confirmation of trust. That is why, in business, he is someone who when he says he'll be there Tuesday at nine and fix the whatever and it'll be $56.00, he'll be there Tuesday at nine and fix the whatever and it'll be $56.00. Go ahead and pay him in advance on the Friday before. He shook your hand; he'll be there and he'll fix it. If a different part is needed, and the total job cost is now $47.50, he'll give you $8.50 back. If it breaks again he'll come back and fix it, make it right for no additional charge. That is how good ol' boys do business; that is why they are good ol' boys. That is the way they were raised, the way it used to be. And with them, that is how it still is. They are out there. They are rare, but they are still out there setting the example for the rest of us to follow. Our best hope is that we all take their lead more often than not.

You know what else good ol' boys have? A sense of humor. Few things are so bad that they can't find something to chuckle about. Being totally serious is not always the answer to everything. There are enough real problems out there without us making it worse on ourselves by frettin' and fidgetin' over every little thing.

Here's some other things good ol' boys do: they open doors for women, help little old ladies and men across the street, say "howdy" to folks, return found wallets, put bandages on kid's skinned knees. They will sit and talk when sitting and talking are what needs to be done.

Something good ol' boys are not always is politically correct. What they are is politely correct, made so by good intentions. They are patriotic, too. Nothing corny, mind you, they just believe in honoring the tradition and sacrifice that has given them their place on this earth, and in this country. When the flag goes by at a parade they stand up and put their right hand over their heart.

You get the picture. A good ol' boy is someone you could invite over for dinner and not worry about the silverware or anything else, who would give you the shirt off his back, who you could trust with your confidences, and is someone who you and other people like to be around. Many will read themselves into being a good ol' boy when in reality there are but a few. But we should all be trying to be one; the world would be a better place for it.

The recipe to make a good ol' boy: start with trust, mix in honesty, then spice it with hard work, common sense, decency, courtesy, and a sense of humor. *Voila!!* Don't think there's anyone like this in real life? There is. The person I have described is my father-in-law.

20
ASSEMBLY INSTRUCTIONS

Assembly instructions? Men don't need them. They put instructions in all those boxes of things that need to be put together for other people, not for men. Men already know how to put things together. It may not always be right, it may take a try or two, but we don't need the instructions because we can, thank you very much, put it together without them. It is a man thing.

All that may sound a little arrogant. It is a little arrogant. Okay, a LOT arrogant. I ask you to forgive us. To explain I have to take you way back to our formative years, to when we were boys. As boys we messed with stuff. Whatever it was, we messed with it. We twisted it, turned it, took it apart and put it back together again. We found old broken things and tried to figure out why they were broken and if we could fix them. We fixed a lot of things by doing that. Maybe not to perfection, but we fixed them. Pretty soon we started thinking we could fix (and do) most anything we put our minds to. Boy arrogance, but not full blown man arrogance yet. We would rather call it the beginnings of confidence.

Take the bicycle. We used it hard. Rough roads, jumps, crashes, showing off. Tires got flat, handle bars got twisted, fenders got bent, nuts and bolts worked their way loose. So we hauled it into the garage, leaned it up on the workbench and went to work. We turned the screws, twisted the handle bars, pounded the dents and patched the tires. We just did those things. Just did them. It was fun. It was satisfying. And, very importantly, we got dirty. Dirty fingernails, dirty faces, and dirty hands, which we wiped on our pants with great glee because dirt is a boy thing. And in all these endeavors, guess what? No instructions. We HAD to figure it out. We were fixit-boys. It just came naturally.

When we were in our early teens and just beginning to feel our strength, our Mom's asked us to open a recalcitrant jar lid, and we did. Yoweeeee! After that she asked us to use the pliers to turn the nut on the washer faucet. And then one day she asked us to put up the new towel bar. And we did. No instructions. We just figured it out. It was getting to be a habit.

Then our Dad took us out to the shop and asked us to change the oil in the tractor while he went to the feed store. All he said was, "Here's the drain plug. Here's where you put the oil in. And here's the oil." Then he left us there to do it, alone, a boy becoming a man. Figure the rest of it out. No written instructions. Just me and the tractor and several quarts of oil between now and a feeling of accomplishment. The drain plug, find a wrench that fits it. A couple of tries and I did. The plug won't budge. I hit the wrench end with a hammer. No dice. I look for a wrench with a longer handle. No luck. I ponder, but I'm not about to say, "Uncle." No way. I spot a piece of two inch pipe, a section about three feet long left over from something or other. Hey, it just might work. I slip the pipe over the wrench and, man, I got another two and a half feet of leverage on that drain plug now. "You're mine, drain plug. I own you," I say to myself. I give it a heave, feeling my new found strength. It budges. It budges! Victory! I give it another pull and it's loose. I take the pipe off the wrench and finish loosening the plug with the wrench alone. I turn the last few turns on the plug with my fingers and pull it out. Oil gets all over me. Awesome! Dirty fingernails, dirty everything. I am at the gates of man land. After the oil drains I put the plug back in and give it that last tug with my wrench-pipe. I put the pipe away for later. It is my friend. I figure that with a long enough pipe I could loosen the nut that holds the world on its axis. And I wouldn't even need instructions to do it. I put the new oil in and the job is done. All I have to wonder about is what the ol' man will ask me to fix next, for surely he will since I did this job so well.

He has seen that I can figure stuff out.

Get the metamorphosis? Men not only don't need assembly instructions, they don't want them. We could save a lot of paper (and trees) if manufacturers would package things for men without the instruction sheet. Just put a label on the outside: "Instructions not included. This box for sale to fixit-men only." Don't think so? Go ahead, pack a Massarati in a box and give us a try. Oops, there goes that arrogance again. But at least now you know where it comes from, and that we come by it honestly. It all started with that old bike, the one we fixed a hundred times. I wonder where that old bike is? I'll bet I could still take it apart and put it back together. Without instructions.

21
COMPRESSORS

Compressors are important in the lives of men. It is not about just having one; it is about the size of the one you have.

Take Jim. He's an abject failure. A complete and total loser. He has no redeeming social value whatsoever. Besides his doting wife, there is no reason he should be walking the face of the earth. None. Except for one thing: his compressor. It is a giant even among giants. Most of us have this little tank with a motor on the top that we push and pull around on wheels and plug into household current. But not Jim. His compressor is on a slab. Permanent. When you walk into his shop, it dominates. It is tall, broad shouldered and barrel chested. There in the corner, I swear it is five stories tall. It is probably five feet, but it seems like five stories. Whatever, it is big. It's a 10,000 psi icon. The motor sits beside it. Also huge, it must be seven-hundred horsepower. Easy. Our compressors plug into 120 volts. Jim's plugs into 220 volts. Rumor has it that it is more like 440 volts because if you want something blown up with air, Jim doesn't flinch. Never. He is totally unafraid in the inflation department. The rest of us inflate our kid's wading pools and an occasional tire, awkwardly trundling our pathetic little average compressors over to the task. But not Jim. When he turns his compressor on, the lights dim. The ground shakes. Seismometers scribble. Women grab their children. Jaws drop, and all mankind within a ten mile radius stops and stares in the direction of Jim's place, "It's Jim again. He's turned on his compressor."

The thing is, Jim's compressor is not only big, he can do so many things with it. He has a long, long hose that reaches any corner of his shop. If one of those earth movers, the kind with the wheels taller than you and with more of them than you can count, came into his driveway, most of us would shudder. Jim just smiles. He smiles a stupid, cocky, self-assured smile. And he gets that look in his eye. THAT look. Like, "Come to Pappa big fella. I'll make it all better. I'll put some pressure on your rims. How much do you want?" He has that much confidence in his compressor. Come to think of it, he could huff and puff and blow your house down if he wanted to.

And tools. Jim has tools that attach to his compressor hose. Tools! The rest of us don't have compressor tools. He'll put his wrench on and he can loosen seven lug nuts quicker than you can say, "Lug nuts." And if you want a demonstration of both his compressor power and his prowess also, he can put them back on faster than you can say, "Nuts lug." Rat-tat-tat. Whiz. Whir. Wham. Jim's tools make all the great sounds. Man sounds. His compressor isn't just a compressor; it's an experience.

So how can such a total loser have such a great compressor? We don't know. Most of us figure he took his daughter's Girl Scout cookie money. Or his son's paper route money. He's a bureaucrat, so we know he doesn't actually earn his money. He doesn't get it from his wife either. She dotes on him right up to the time he reaches for the checkbook. Then dote turns to, "Touch that and I'll break your arm." No, he didn't buy it with her money. Oh hell, who cares how he got it? So what if he held up Chase-Manhattan? He's still got it. He can still put out enough psi to inflate the universe, enough ratchety sounds to put the rest of us in therapy for inadequacy. While us average guys are compressor impaired, he remains compressor rich.

So why do we hang around Jim? Why does he have friends at all if he is such an abject loser? It is his compressor. We become greater by association. So why is he still a total reject in the eyes of mankind? We are jealous. There, I said it. Jealous. I'll say it again: jealous, jealous, jealous. It's out. It's almost therapeutic.

What else can we be of someone who has the most awesome compressor west of the Mississippi? Only thing we can do to save any shred of dignity is to label him a sorry sumbitch. So we do. It makes us feel better. Jim's feelings? Who cares? This is man land, remember? But sometimes even all that isn't enough. I swear, whenever Jim is down, he just goes out to his shop and turns on his compressor, and then all is right with the world. And the rest of us become mere mortals.

Okay. He's not such a bad guy. And I'll tell you something else about Jim. He'll be your friend. For cheap. For $3.99. Buy him a six pack and he'll be your friend for life. Besides, hang around him enough and he might even let you turn on his compressor. After all is said and done, that makes him OK in man land.

22
MAN PHILOSOPHY

Most man philosophy is succinct, occasionally even opinion-ated (imagine that). But it all comes from the heart . . . and the gut. Some examples:

If all else fails, go fishin'.

* * *

No clothes are so dirty that they can't be worn one more day.

* * *

Perspiration is good. Sweat is better.

* * *

Wimpy truck equals wimpy guy.

* * *

It's okay to be a man doing man things.

* * *

If you're gonna be a jerk, do it around the guys. They expect it.

Any new project is worth buying a new tool for.

* * *

It's okay to treat a woman like a lady.

* * *

Men don't like men who are jerks around women any better than women like men who are jerks around women.

* * *

You'll ". . . do it next week" will fly a lot better than ". . . I'll get to it later."

* * *

Wash the dishes once in awhile. It's a great way to get the fingernails clean.

* * *

To keep your blue jeans manly, hide them so they won't get found and washed.

* * *

Inside every business suit is a man wanting out.

* * *

You can't have too many tools.

* * *

Truth is to be found where the workin' man works.

* * *

Talking to the guy at the auto body shop is pretty near as good as doin' the job yourself.

If you meet a girl who says she changes her own oil, check her fingernails. She might just be trying another one of those phony come-ons.

* * *

Don't waste time deciding. Just wear what's on top when you open the dresser drawer.

* * *

Too much thinkin' ain't good for you.

* * *

What the world needs is more participants and fewer bureaucrats.

* * *

The trouble with politics is that spin is often more important than truth.

* * *

A politician who tries to be everything to everyone ends up being nothing to nobody.

* * *

Bad is a small car going downhill slow in the left lane with an eighteen wheeler right behind it.

* * *

Outside Christmas lights need to be taken down by the first day of summer.

* * *

Individual responsibility is a damn sight better than a bevy of government protecto-crats.

* * *

Domestic job security is a project unfinished.

You can't change *the* world, but you can make a difference in *your* world.

* * *

Workers know more than bosses. That's why the best bosses are people who listen.

* * *

Back when women . . . you really didn't think I was going to finish that sentence, did you?

* * *

If you show a copy of *Man Things,* admission to "Plowers Anonymous" is free.

* * *

It'd be darn boring if we were all the same.

* * *

Best way to stay in a good mood is to not listen to the news.

* * *

Rhetoric will never conquer substance.

* * *

An old car well kept is better than a new car ill kept.

* * *

Buy Girl Scout cookies.

* * *

Earning something is better than demanding it.

* * *

The trouble with critics is that they are so critical.

A coward is a renter of life, owning no character of his own.

* * *

Lamenting your fate delivers you not from it.

* * *

Wealth is not the right of government, but of the people.

* * *

Continually blaming others for your misfortunes is living a lie.

* * *

Style goes out of style. Class doesn't.

* * *

Most all of mankind's successes can be traced to his perseverance. Most all his failures can be traced to his excesses.

* * *

The best pleasures are simple pleasures.

* * *

Life is not a thing. It is a process.

* * *

Create a life of honor. Do not live a life of envy.

* * *

Handouts don't make your life better, only more dependent.

We may be created equal, but we do not labor equally.

* * *

Teach your children to live, rather than obtain.

* * *

Wisdom is the result of victories *and* defeats.

* * *

Create simplicity, then savor it.

* * *

A society is only as good as its families.

* * *

If you are not willing to defend what you believe in, then what you believe in will die.

* * *

Fixing blame is not the solution to every problem.

* * *

Criticism is easier than involvement. That's why there is so much criticism.

* * *

The efforts of the few should not be depleted by the lethargy of the many.

* * *

A child who has never experienced love can never pass it on.

* * *

One problem with politics is that ego is often greater than ability.

Any politician whose primary motivation is re-election should not be re-elected.

* * *

A study of our civilization a thousand years hence will reveal that it pretty much revolved around grams of fat.

* * *

Greg Hess' name has been in every book I've ever written. I just kept the string alive.

* * *

If the Wright brothers had listened to the advice of their day, they would not have flown.

* * *

Football is testosterone displayed on a green background.

* * *

More important than being smart is being kind.

* * *

A society of honor is better than a society that honors possessions.

* * *

There are studies that justify every behavior. That doesn't justify every behavior.

* * *

Character solves more problems than money.

* * *

Life is like a book. You create it one chapter at a time.

If you are wearing something that has to be dry cleaned, you are dressed up.

* * *

Life isn't about worrying. It's about doing.

* * *

There is much about nothing in life: lighten up.

* * *

Happiness is family watching a sunrise on a mountain lake.

23
DUMP TRUCKS AND MODEL TRAINS

Now get down and get into this with me. Dump trucks and model trains are man things. The reason is, they come naturally.

I had this dump truck when I was a boy. Metal. No plastic. Yellow cab and green dump bed. I steered it with the horn on the hood; turn the horn and the front wheels turned. It was awesome. Pull the lever beside the dump bed and the bed dumped. The tailgate flipped open, too. Load, haul, and dump. I spent hours doing that. I had this favorite hillside with soft dirt. I made great roads there. Loaded, hauled, and dumped. I steered with the horn, crawling alongside the truck on my knees, making truck sounds. And, if I do say so myself, I made great truck sounds: down shifted, up shifted, with occasional screeches when I had to come to a sudden halt. I was happy. Beats the heck out of growing up surrounded by graffiti.

Now a grown man, I still covet dump trucks. I come by it naturally. I have one all picked out, too, for when I win the lottery. It sits on this big truck lot I drive by on the way to work. It is white, sits up high with a great expanse of hood. It has a gray dump bed, sitting atop some big duals. It probably has twenty-seven speeds forward and five in reverse. It is totally impressive. I am sure it will make the correct amount of man noise, a deep rumble. The whole thing kind of makes you all tingly, doesn't it?

I have driven it in my dreams, experienced the beauty that is driving a dump truck. You get to drive on-road and off-road. Eighteen wheelers are okay, but they are rather straight-line pavement-rigs. A dump truck is the best of all worlds. With a dump truck you get to load and unload in a hurry. Very little waiting around means more dump truck driving. It is a nifty concept.

Watch for me right after I win the lottery. I will be the guy in the new dump truck with the big smile on his face. I'm going to drive it to my favorite Mexican restaurant, Pedro's La Margarita in Salem, Oregon (best Mexican food in the galaxy). My wife may or may not be in the cab with me. More than likely not. She will be in the car, several cars back, looking everywhere but at the dump truck. I know what my kids will say, too, "We'll meet you down there a little later, Dad." But in the morning, when we drive it to "Plowers Anonymous," they'll say, "Can I drive it, Dad?" Once you pass the age of being self-conscious about it, you can be really happy in man land.

I had a fine model train as a boy. I played with it a lot. Knew exactly how to do it, too. It is genetic. It had coal cars, cattle cars, caboose, a station, and even an engine that puffed smoke. Straight track, curved track, and a trestle to boot. When my train set-up overflowed my bedroom, it spilled out into the living room. Folks just stepped around it, unless company was coming. Then I had to re-route. When a train disappears around the corner of a wall and then comes back to you, you are a boy in control, a master of construction. It is like a primer on man things. When you are playing train, you spend a lot of time on your hands and knees. You have to get down to where the train is happening to really get into it.

I still have a train. I set it up every Christmas, around the base of the tree. That is my job. (I tried tree decorating once, but it got re-done.) I do my train setting-up job real well. I go way back with toy trains. I still get down on my hands and knees. I just get up a little slower.

The fact that toy trains are part of the male genetic make-up was brought home to me recently when my in-laws came to our house for Christmas. While my mother-in-law stood back and admired her daughter's tree, guess what my father-in-law did? He dropped down on his seventy-five-year-old knees and played train.

He took hold of the transformer and ran the train forward, changed the switch, backed up, unhooked, pulled back on the main track, re-switched, and ran the train around the track. I'm not sure where he learned how to play train. He didn't even have electricity where he grew up, but he dang sure knew how. It was a beautiful thing to watch. It was man poetry.

Man land has room for lots of man toys.

24
MEAT LOAF SANDWICH

I am not sure this is exclusively a man thing. But it is in my house.

Do you ever arrive home late at night after everyone in the family has gone to bed? I do, quite often, after a long trip. The first thing I do is open the fridge. If I find some left over meat loaf, I am immediately in my happy place. The house is all quiet and dimly lit, so peaceful. Whatever rough edges I have left over from the day, the calming effect of the quiet at home smoothes them out. And the thought of a meat loaf sandwich late at night takes them away altogether.

You set all the stuff out: white bread, mayonnaise, ketchup, and the meat loaf. No frills. It is pure and it is simple. You make it right there on the counter, mayonnaise on one slice of bread, and ketchup on the other. Then you cut a couple of big ol' thick chunks of meat loaf and slap the bread around them. *Voila!* Man gourmet. You don't sit down, just put the sandwich in one hand and a napkin for the dripping in the other. If it doesn't drip you didn't make it right. Then stroll slowly around the house.

While strolling and munching, you think of the wonderful things that have taken place in your house over the years. Look at the dining table, all quiet now. But remember the time Uncle Rusty told about escaping from a German POW camp during World War II. He hid in a corn silo until he couldn't stand the smell of the rotting corn any more. When he came out, he got re-captured. He escaped again. He said that during the end of the war, the Germans became kinder. One day while he was running and hiding, there was an air raid siren. When that happened all the German citizens would head for their cellars. Uncle Rusty was hungry. During the raid he sneaked into a local farm house. The occupants had been having lunch and there was bread on the table. Uncle Rusty took all of it. He wonders to this day what those people thought when they came back to their table after the air raid and their bread was missing.

I take another bite and chew it slowly while remembering when my Mom's friend, Vernell, sat at that table and told about the time in 1914, when he was seven years old and all the way home from school one day, a four mile walk, all he could think about was the twenty-five cent piece he had hidden in his room. He'd had it there for a month. When he arrived home he got the quarter out of its hiding place. He saddled his horse, rode seven miles to the store and bought five candy bars. On the way home, he ate every one of them. It was a rare treat.

I keep munching and wander into the living room and look at the corner where the Christmas tree goes. I remember the first red two-wheeler we got our son for Christmas. I remember the look on his face. I remember, too, the time I had a picture my wife painted framed. She was so surprised that Christmas morning and the picture looked so good. She couldn't imagine her artwork could look that good. The framing brought home the fact that she does great work.

And I remember a dinner party we had. After dinner, we all gathered in the living room and my wife offered and served everyone an after dinner liqueur. Everyone that is, except Peggy. She had overlooked her. But Peggy wasn't going to be overlooked. With all the wisdom and grace of her eighty-four years, she said to my wife, "Do you believe I would like one of those?" Everyone roared. I have never seen anything handled better. My wife said, "Why, yes, I believe you would."

Two thirds of the sandwich is gone now and I wander back to the breakfast nook and remember a story my father-in-law had told.

As a young boy, he was driving a team of horses that were pulling a wagon which hauled grain bundles to the stationary thrasher. He was twelve years old. The old farmers told him he couldn't be a man unless he took a chew of tobacco. So he took a chew of tobacco. Then he had to unload the wagon. The only problem was the tobacco made him sicker than a dog. But he wasn't about to let on. He unloaded in record time, drove the wagon over to a tree and dove off, sicker than a blowed-up chicken. He was a man. He never chewed again.

And I look in the kitchen and think of the time when Lucy and Al came over for dinner. They are such wonderful people that you just smile when you think about them. When things got hectic in the kitchen, Al took over sauteing the mushrooms. I can still see him there, talking and laughing like he always does. The kitchen is quiet now. But the memories linger.

This is the stuff of life. This is what we savor, what makes it all worthwhile. This is stuff about the people we love. And I think about it on those occasions when I can slow down, reflect, and remember. For me that is late at night, in my home, with a meat loaf sandwich. Without the sandwich I just go to bed. The sandwich is the whole thing. It is my secret man thing.

25
COILING

I am going to go out on a limb and I am probably going to take some hits for it. I am going to tell you about something women cannot do. (Just reading that kinda perks your ears up, doesn't it?) Women can do anything on the face of this earth but they cannot coil hoses. Or ropes. Or electrical cords. It's the dang truth. I don't know why they can't, but they just can't. None of them can. My wife says they can, they just don't want to. That may be true (I'll have to take her word for it) and if it is then I'll have to modify my statement: Women don't coil hoses because they don't want to coil hoses. Or ropes. Or electrical cords. Whatever. The fact still remains that they don't. If it weren't for men, every hose in every neighborhood would be strewn across the lawns of America, every rope would be in a ball, and every electrical cord in a pile. Now that's a pretty strong statement. I will back it up.

When a man comes home and sees the hose strung across the lawn going to a flower bed and no one is in sight, he knows instinctively that his wife is through working in the yard for the day and it is up to him to coil the hose. Some of it may be his own fault. One time she did "coil" the hose. Thing was, only fifty percent of it was coiled. The rest of it was in figure eights. Unacceptable. Unacceptable in man land. Hose coiling in man land requires all kinks to be out and the hose resting in a smoothly coiled position. He gently mentioned this fact once to his wife and she mentioned to him, not so gently, that he was free to coil it any way he wanted.

She also suggested a place he could put it, but it wasn't very practical. So now when he comes home and sees the hose across the lawn he knows he is free to coil it any way he wants. And he does.

Personally, I solved the hose coiling problem by buying one of those hose coiling things, the kind where you just turn the handle and the hose rolls right up onto the reel. My wife loves it. So do I. I had previously tried hose hanging brackets. No good. I got figure eights there, too. No, the hose reel thing with the handle is the best device, by far, for outside domestic tranquillity.

About ropes. I'm talking about boat ropes that you use to tie to the dock and pull skiers. They all have to be rolled up right or they don't fit into all those little boat compartments. And because if you don't roll them up right, the next time you go to use them, half your recreational day is spent un-knotting them. But no, women pile them. Just pile them. Sometimes it works and they unpile nicely. And sometimes they don't. Men prefer they work nicely every time, so they coil them carefully. But it is not a huge deal because putting the boat away is a man thing. And putting the boat away means re-coiling all the ropes properly. It is part of the man ritual. That way the next time you go boating you know the ropes are ready.

Electrical cords are a big deal. Electrical cords are used and re-used in all sorts of situations. They are the umbilical to a man's power tools, so they have to be ready. To be ready means they have to be coiled properly. It is like my friend Patrick talks about. When he uses the cord he unrolls what he needs, uses it, then coils it back up. His wife unrolls the whole thing no matter how much she needs, uses it, then leaves it. He goes to pull in the garage and can't because there is one hundred and fifty feet of electrical cord piled in the middle of the floor. It is in coils, figure eights, two square knots, a bowline, and a triple-toe-loop-double-axle. It takes him three days but he gets it coiled back up. It is his man duty. His duty complete, he can pull his truck back in the garage. When he goes into the house he doesn't say anything about the electrical cord. It is just understood that's his job. It is understood that it is every man's job.

Coiling

There are some things in this life that you just have to accept, that you just have to sit back, shrug, and say, "That's the way it is." Men doing the coiling is one of those things.

26
MUFFLER 101

Every man knows the moral of this story. The other half of the population may or may not. So it is time to shout it out: "All you need are a few simple hand tools and thirty minutes time" is a lie. A big fat lie. Every man knows it because every man has been there. It looks good on the outside of the box—it sells good—but it never quite works that way. A "few simple hand tools" includes that left-handed over-center re-ratcheting titanium reinforced moon rock buster that only one specialty store in all the U.S. of A. has, for $750.00 on sale, when they can get it. Right now they can't. It is back ordered for three years. It is a "simple hand tool" for the guy that wrote the script on the box because he has one. He inherited it five years ago and it is now displayed on his fireplace mantle for all to see. But it is not a simple hand tool and we all know it. It is just a man fact of life when doing projects.

"Thirty minutes time" is also a lie. Take whatever number they give you and multiply it by ten. The "thirty minute" figure came from a test they did on a standard atmosphere day, seventy-two degrees Fahrenheit, calm, dry, all required tools within fingertip reach and the old 'whatever' already removed. All the test-assembler had to do, after they said, "Ready, set, go," was grab a tool, strap on the part, tighten here and there and, bingo, a twenty-seven minute job. They round the twenty-seven up to thirty to show what great guys they are.

Now let's visit reality. Let's install a muffler. That is a man thing; it is under the car. Under the car is a man place (if not THE man place). The muffler box says, "... a few simple hand tools and thirty minutes time." It is time for the truth, and since this is educational we'll call it 'Muffler 101.'

First of all, the old muffler won't come off. Not easily, anyway. It is rusted all around the hole it has in it. That rust falls in your face while you are under the car pondering the job. The clamps are rusted and you can't get any kind of wrench within one foot of the nuts because something obstructs the access every way you try it. You bump your head and knuckles a lot. See? It takes thirty minutes to install but what they didn't tell you about was taking the old one off. You started at nine and it is now ten thirty and you haven't progressed. You've spent an hour and twenty pondering and trying and ten minutes swearing (head and knuckles, remember?) and . . . nothing accomplished. You do not give up.

On to bigger and better tools. On to tools that break things. The old muffler *will* come off. The car may never be the same, but the muffler WILL come off. You spray Liquid Wrench on the recalcitrant muffler clamps. Your wife pokes her head into the garage and smells the aroma and says, "Smells like man stuff out here." Liquid Wrench is to dissolve the rust to make it easier to get the clamps off. You wish it would dissolve the clamps totally or, if things don't get better, the car. Whatever, you are moving on to the pry bar. Wedge it in around the clamps and reef on it (that's man talk for "pull hard"). Reef on it real hard. All finesse is out the window now. You are on a mission to show the old muffler who is boss. Reefing works. Almost. The old rusted clamp bends: One small victory for muffler-repair-man. But it doesn't break. It is time for the really big tool: the bolt cutter. Nothing stops the bolt cutter. You crawl back under the car and get hold of the clamp with the 'big tool' and, bingo, you cut it. The clamp falls off. It is gone, history. It gave up. You win. One more cut on the other clamp and it is gone, too. Victory! All clamps are gone. No going back now. It is either get it done or be without a car. You are darn sure not going to limp on down to Midas and say, "Uh, you mind finishing this job?" You are in serious man land now. Defeat is not a part of the program.

Not everything is totally difficult. Some things go according to plan: The muffler hangers come off without much difficulty. A 7/16" box wrench here and a 1/2" open-end wrench there and the muffler and tail pipe are free. Wriggle it on out from under the car and lay it on the floor in front of you. The monster is exposed. You tamed it. It only took you three hours.

Time to get to work on removing the muffler from the tailpipe. At least it is out on the floor where you can get to it easy. That is half the battle. That is another way they come up with that "thirty minutes." They put the car up on a hoist. They just don't tell you that.

You didn't figure on new clamps. Figured you'd use the old ones. But you had to destroy them to save the project. Destruction is better than admitting defeat. So you plan on at least one more trip to the parts store. That is about average for most man projects, one more trip than you figured. The "thirty minute" guy has a parts store in his back room.

You saw the old tailpipes off, remove the old muffler, slide the new muffler on the old tailpipes, put on the new clamps and reinstall. Easy. Almost a thirty minute job, right? Wrong. While sawing the old tailpipe your one blade for sawing metal breaks. Snap! Dangit! It's off to the hardware store. Leave the coveralls on. You get better service that way; people in coveralls know what they are doing. You go to the saw blade aisle. Let's see, should we get the one super-duper-forever blade for $9.00 or the pack of four, resists breaking, cuts quarter inch steel, for $7.00? Get the four. More tools is always better. You also get the two new clamps at the parts store on the way home.

Okay, you are now ready to finish and declare total victory. Except that the new saw blade breaks while cutting. What the heck's going on? Try some lubricant, go slower. Patience may be a virtue, but it is not always a man thing while in project-land. It works this time, though. You saw halfway through and bend the pipe and it breaks clean. You cut the other end and break another blade. Slow down. More lubricant. It works. The cutting is complete and the old muffler removed. You eyeball the culprit then toss it aside in ceremonial victory.

Project completion is near. You grind the old tailpipe ends to smooth their edges. Grinding is good. It is noisy, makes sparks, and you get to wear goggles. Man stuff. Four and a half hours later you pull the new muffler out of the box that said, ". . . few simple hand tools and thirty minutes." The muffler is pretty. It is new and un-rusted. And it is guaranteed until the sun don't shine. You tap the old tailpipes on and clamp on the clamps. They are new so they snug up good. Assembly complete, it is time to admire it a little. Shiny new muffler about ready to go on under the car and last about five years. That is about how long "guaranteed for life" mufflers last. And it is time to be glad you did not have to put in a new exhaust pipe. Those things have to be bent every which way to fit. Today the old one works just fine.

Slide the assembly under the car. You hope it fits. An inch off here or there and it won't work. The muffler/tailpipe assembly has to match up with the hangers or you are SOL. As luck would have it, today you're not SOL. It fits. It takes a little wiggling and banging and a few colorful words, but it fits. Okay, okay, so it didn't fit perfectly. Making it fit is just as good as an exact fit in man land. Another grunt and groan or so, a wrench here and there to snug things up, a little more rust and dirt in the face and . . . project complete.

Now it is time to lay there and look at it, to touch and wiggle it. It is new and pretty. It is solid. It is art work. YOU did it. Not Midas. Not Joe's Muffler. Not Topeka Exhaust . . . with all their tools and hoists and stuff . . . but you! And you did it for $25.95 (not including clamps and broken saw blades) as opposed to $225.95. Bargains are important to men, especially the kind that happen because of their man skill and perseverance.

So it took you five hours, but you did it. That's about right: thirty minutes times ten equals three hundred minutes equals five hours. Right on schedule. And you did it with a few simple hand tools, after the pry bar, bolt cutter and extra saw blades. Those box instructions lie, but men know that. Now everybody knows it.

27
CAMPING

When a man goes camping you may think he just wants to be outdoors, to set up the tent and cook on the camp stove. It is those things, but it is a lot more. Camping is a reaffirmation of what runs deep in a man's psyche: survival. Pure . . . raw . . . survival. Man instinct. Let's explore it.

When a man steps outside his tent in the morning it appears he is just breathing fresh air and looking skyward to see the pine trees sway in the light breeze to the background of blue sky and puffy white clouds. Externally, he is. Internally he is surveying the territory. This is *his* territory to *survive* on. That is the way it has been since time immemorial. His glance skyward is a summoning of the strength for the survival challenge. In his psyche a man has to know that he can survive without the tent, that he could construct a lean-to shelter from the materials around him, that he could sleep on a pine bough bed in his buckskin outfit. He also has to know that he could find food, and mark and defend his territory. Modern camping is but a catalyst for his deeper instincts.

Take food. Sure he can cook a souffle on his camp stove to rival the best restaurant in San Francisco. But as he cooks the souffle, look deep into his eyes. What he is really doing is providing sustenance and proving he can provide it in the wild. He could cook on a fire on the ground if he had to, throw raw meat on the coals, turn it, sear it, and then pull it out of the fire and scrape away the char, cool it and eat it. He could eat it with his hands, tearing it by biting and pulling and spitting the ashes and dirt and biting and pulling and tearing some more, probably squatting on his haunches all the while. To the outside observer he may *look* like he is sitting at the space-age-all-aluminum-micro-folding-authentic-imitation-wood grain camp table, but in his mind he is squatting and tearing and spitting, because he knows what it takes to survive in the elements. He is confirming that he could survive in the wilderness if he had to.

It is the same thing on the floor of the stock market, men shouting and scratching and clawing. They are surviving. The shelter may be a bit more sophisticated, the methodology different, but the principal is the same.

A man has to mark his territory while camping. Men generally eschew those port-a-potty things. Trees are much preferred. Mark 'em. If it is good enough for wolves, it is good enough for man.

A man also must be able to defend and protect. He will glance skyward again to summon the strength for the defense. He has his territory, has marked it with rocks and scent, and now stands ready to defend his kind, his family, and what he stands for.

No, camping is not just camping. I have shown that with a peek into the inner psyche of man. It is *survival*. A man camping is a survivor in the wilderness and a hero for the ages.

28
FOOTBALL

What is it about football and men? What about all the yelling and jumping up and down and the clenching of fists and fervor and intensity? Football is competition with rules on a battlefield with boundaries. For that reason it is fun to observe. I will explain at the end of the chapter.

Football is blood and guts and power and finesse and strength and guile and standing up and getting knocked down and standing up again and knocking someone else down and working as a team for the objective of scoring and getting scored upon but getting the opportunity to score upon the other guy and about not giving up and about grinding it out or going end-around or the quick strike long pass and being called for infractions and getting away with a few infractions and about risk and reward and looking out for your buddy and your buddy looking out for you and the victory thrill and the defeat agony but about being able to play again another day and about rules and boundaries and planning and precision and preparation and speed and smarts and reading the defense and planning the offense and supporting those who support you and about continuing even when it hurts and overcoming obstacles and never giving up and never giving up and never giving up and sharing victory with others and giving credit to others for your victories and about sharing defeat but blaming no one and about belonging and working together for a common goal and about keeping it all in perspective as in getting thrown for a loss does not mean you can't make a big gain on the next play and about finding out the harder you work the better things go for you and even if they don't you never stop trying because effort is what it is all about and because you are hit at the line of scrimmage you bounce back and hit it again and get some gain where there was none and you get money and reward and a sense of accomplishment to play and because afterwards you get to go and take a long hot shower and go home and hug your family and relax because that is what it is all about.

Now go back and re-read the last paragraph, except for the first word "football" substitute the word "life."

That is why men like football. It is life displayed on a green background in one three hour sitting. On a given day some win, some lose, but all should keep playing the game. As long as you keep playing, you are a winner. That is what life is all about.

29
MAN PACKS

My oldest son is of the age where some of his friends are getting married. He attended a post-wedding gift-opening party in honor of his friend Adam. After Adam watched his new bride open several gifts of towels and linens and silver platters and frilly things, all of which he appreciated, he made the comment, "You know what I think they need to make? A man pack." The males in attendance nodded, as Adam's wife opened a package containing a beautiful lace table cloth. It was all very nice.

When my son got home he related the story to me. I thought a "man pack" was a darn good idea. So we set out to design one. First of all, it comes in a big wooden box. At the beginning of the gift opening we would set it at Adam's feet and while all the foo-foo stuff was happening he would reach in and find great joy in all the things inside. Here's what he would find:

- coveralls
- tool belt
- hammer
- socket set
- case of oil
- oil filter wrench
- cordless drill
- shovel

- crow bar
- grease gun
- plaid flannel shirt
- tractor logo ball cap
- caulk
- circuit tester
- stud finder
- skill saw
- gift certificate to "Auto Zone"
- screwdrivers
- duct tape
- more screwdrivers
- lots of electrical tape
- more screwdrivers
- bucket
- leather gloves
- a "how to" book (he won't need it but he can loan it)

———————

Now *that* is a gift to put Adam in his happy place. It would transform a very nice event into an awesome happening. You know it follows that they would live happily ever after. In reality it is too late to give Adam his "man pack." He got married before they were invented. But he planted the idea and he has a twin brother, not yet married. Aaron, you are a lucky man. You can expect a "man pack."

30
TOOL BOX

You can tell a lot about a man by his tool box. You really can. It is very nearly a map of his life. Go with a man to his tool box and ask him about its contents. He will tell you those are not just a bunch of tools in there. They are a bunch of memories, too. My tool box is one of those big, red roll around kind. The lower level is for the big stuff and the upper level is for everything else. In it is all my stuff and a lot of memories.

I didn't always have a big red tool box. As a boy my first tools were an "Outboard Marine Tool Kit." I got it for my birthday. There were three plastic pouches that held a screwdriver, pliers, and some open-end wrenches. You folded the pouches and tied a strap around to hold it all together. The screwdriver was a red-handled Phillips. I still have it. I open the screwdriver drawer in my tool box and there are twenty-eight screwdrivers in there—all shapes, sizes, and kinds (remember, you can't have too many tools)—but I always gravitate to the old red handled Phillips. Somehow it is usually on top. If it is a Phillips I need, it is the one I use. It is my sentimental favorite.

There is another special screwdriver in there. It was given to me by a very good friend who died young (fifty-two) of lung cancer. My wife and I went to his bedside every day during his last months in the hospital. He had been a pilot in World War II, flew B-25's. Steve was his name. Steve gave me a kind of screwdriver you can't buy any more. It is a flat-head made of one piece of steel with wood

117

(*real* wood) attached to the sides as handles. It is very old. It is very durable. I use it a lot. It is very special.

The shiny sockets strewn all over the removable tray in the top of my tool box are some of my first. When we were first married we didn't have much money. And I didn't have very many tools. Then an ad arrived in the mail for an entire tool box and tools! A jillion different tools (one-hundred-seventy-six to be exact) complete with the box, for $39.95. Didn't have $39.95. Ordered it anyway. It was my turn. Just the previous month my wife had purchased a one-hundred-seventy-six piece set of dishes for $39.95. With these two purchases we would have everything. The tool box came. It was dented but that didn't matter. There were a jillion tools inside. Mine! Some of the stuff was not what you would call "high quality" and has since faded away (like the dishes). But the sockets, curiously enough, were quite good. And quite shiny. That is why I still recognize them. They are still shiny. And they were from my first major tool purchase.

The ratchet handle for the sockets is becoming a little loosey-goosey. But it is twenty-something years old and still hangin' in there. Old tools are kinda like old soldiers: "They never die; they just fade away."

My folks gave me the metric sockets so I could keep my venerable '59 Volkswagen Beetle running. I didn't need metric before that. Even my $39.95 jillion piece set didn't have any metric stuff. But everything is metric now so I always appreciate my folks when I use those metric sockets.

Wrenches. There are lots of them. Open end, box, crescent, pipe, etc. Those you seem get one at a time, after you get the most important two: a one-half inch open-end on one end and box on the other, and a three-quarter inch, same kind. Those two have been to 75% of my projects over the years, be it metal, wood, washing machine, tricycle, or space age plastic. No man can go through life without those two wrenches. The twenty five or so other wrenches just accumulated around those two.

The 10" crescent wrench? Found it. I was in the Air Force a bunch of years back, down in Texas. One day I went jogging on a dirt back road. It was hotter than hell. Something shiny along side the road caught my eye. I stopped. It was a 10" crescent wrench. There was no one in sight and, hey, it was a tool. I sure wasn't going to leave it there. Those horny toads didn't have any use for it. So I picked it up and jogged the three miles home carrying it in one hand. Actually I changed hands quite a bit. I earned that wrench. But, in my heart, I still know it's not mine. It has the letter "B" engraved on the handle. "B" if you read this, you can have your wrench back. I'm sure you miss it. A 10" crescent wrench feels good in your hand. If it's any consolation, it has a good home. I use it on the propane tank fitting on the barbecue whenever it needs refilling. That wrench is responsible for many a fine barbecue.

Then there is the old pipe wrench. And I do mean old. It is all rusted, heavy as sin and barely works. I finally had to go man shopping at the hardware store a couple of years back and get a new one. But I still have the old one. Some tools may fade away, but you darn sure don't *throw* them away. That's NOT a man thing! Where did I get that old pipe wrench? I don't have a clue.

There are a couple other kinds of wrenches, too: spoke and spark plug. Man, I fixed a lot of the kids—mine and the neighbors—bicycle wheels with those spoke wrenches. Twist out the old and twist in the new, then watch them ride off glad and happy. Tools are good for the heart. I don't have grandkids, but if I ever do and they bring their bicycles over I will be ready. So will my heart.

The spark plug wrench. I bought my first one for the first piece of equipment I ever purchased, a lawn mower. It was a rotary, 20", push, with a 3.5 HP Briggs and Stratton. I had to buy it. Six weeks after my wife and I were married, the Air Force moved us into a house that had grass around it. If you have to buy something it is easier if it has a motor on it. I took fine care of that mower. That is why I bought the spark plug wrench, so I could keep fresh plugs in it. My mower got left out in the rain once. I looked outside and told my wife, "My mower has tears in its carburetor." (That may have been her very first clue that she was in for a long haul with my man things.) After the rain the mower missed a bit while running. So I used my spark plug wrench to put in a new spark plug. Not long after, it started missing again. I used my spark plug wrench and took the new plug out and put the old one back in. It is still in, twenty-five years later. Champion CJ8.

Speaking of the long haul, I still have the same wife and the same mower . . . engine. The rest of the mower eventually rotted away, but I still have the engine. I am going to run it again someday, too. With the same spark plug. I am going to take the plug out and clean it first. I'll take it out with my very first spark plug wrench. It's still right there in the top of my tool box.

One other kind of wrench, too: ignition. I have a bunch of them. I've never used them, but I have them. In man land, possession is as important as use. I don't use them because I am not that great an auto mechanic. I'm okay, but not great. My Uncle Rusty is great. He can fix anything. He can use ignition wrenches. They are for fine work. But he has never had occasion to use mine and neither have I. But they are in there and they look good. My wife is always decorating with flowers and hangings and potpourri, so why can't I? That's it. My ignition wrenches are tool box potpourri.

Tucked in the side of one of the tool box drawers is a yellow, wooden extension rule, the kind you fold and unfold. Real wood. Says "Lufkin extension rule" and "Made in USA" on it. I'm not even sure you can still buy one. It was Uncle Dewell's, on my wife's side. He was a master craftsman. Of course it was made in the USA. It was made a long time ago.

Tool boxes are not just about tools. They are also about the remnants of past projects that get put in there. And about a lot of other stuff that gets put in there, too. That little two inch octagonal piece of metal? It was a hub cap off the right rear tire of our kids first tricycle, yellow one with the black seat that had "World Champion Ankle Biter Bull Rider" stenciled on it. That rotor tucked over in the corner of the bottom drawer is from the distributor of my first car, the '59 VW. Great car. I've loved Beetles ever since. The orange touch-up paint applicator was for my orange '76 Datsun pickup, long gone now. The radiator cap was for the repair we did on my oldest son's first car. That car is long gone now, too. The hammer head is from my first hammer. Yes, I'm going to replace the handle on it—wooden—one of these days. And then I'll hang it back up on the wall behind my work bench. That rusted old sink drain I salvaged from my in-laws' lake cabin that burned down. It was the cabin where my wife and I spent our honeymoon. That equally rusted old lug wrench? That's another story: Some people came into my wife's office one day, said they had a flat tire but had no lug wrench and needed to borrow one. My wife is a very caring person, a good Samaritan (that's how they raise 'em in West Texas), so she loaned the people her lug wrench. She then went back into her office. Of course after the people fixed their tire they just took off. Took the lug wrench, too. But because my wife is a caring person she has lots of friends, including ones on the police force. One day, when one of her police friends came in her office, she reported the lug wrench caper to him. Three weeks later he returned and said, "We had the entire force on this. Finally got it solved." He then gave her this old, decrepit, rusted lug wrench. It was in an evidence bag. It wasn't *the* lug wrench, but it was *a* lug wrench. It's still in the evidence bag and it's still in my toolbox. I'm afraid to use it, afraid it might crumble or something. But I'm not going to throw it away. It's a memory.

There is a screen door tool in my tool box, too, that you use to re-screen sliding patio doors. I used it once to repair the neighbor lady's door. I'm not sure I did that great a job, but I tried. She's a widow and a very nice lady. There's also a wheel puller. Got that to pull a flywheel off something that I sold before I got to pull the flywheel off. But if I ever need one I still have the wheel puller. That's like the power pull I got. There it was right in front of me at the hardware store, on sale. So I bought it. Didn't need it, just bought it. It stayed in its box, still in the cellophane wrapping, for three years. But when I had a gate that needed bracing, guess what the tool of choice was? I took the cellophane off and put that tool right to work. It was great. It fit the man dictum: "When you gotta have the tool you gotta have the tool."

There are a lot of windshield wipers stuffed in the tool box, from cars past and from purchases the didn't fit. They will fit something some day. And there's a lot of oil filter wrenches, because only about fifty percent of the oil filter wrenches you buy actually work. They are all made with some neat, foolproof idea. It's just that in actual practice they don't work, or don't fit where they have to fit. A grave yard of oil filter wrenches is just a man fact of life. But they are still in the tool box. They might fit something some day.

The very first pocket knife my Dad gave me is in there. It is pretty well worn, a little rusted, and not much good any more. But it's going to stay in the tool box, top left drawer. So is that big button I saved off of some coat. Don't know which coat, but it was probably off some favorite work coat or something. Why save the button? Hey, it's my tool box. I don't have to have a reason for everything. If you must know, saving it is better than throwing it away. Man logic.

The newest tool in my tool box is a "Quick Grip." My youngest son gave it to me and it is really nifty. It has a pistol-type grip that you squeeze and the two padded ends come together to grip and hold whatever you want to grip and hold. It is smooth, gentle, easy to use and easy to release. And it just goes to show you that men must constantly be on the look out for new tools. My tool box is not totally full. There is always room for more tools. And, from where we started this discussion, even if there are a lot of great memories in that tool box, there's always room for more.

31
HUNTING

———————

I don't hunt. (I never said all men do all man things; they sort of pick and choose.) I used to hunt, but not any more. But I understand the man concept and the man feelings (instincts?) behind hunting. I have experienced them.

We used to hunt deer on the farm. We hunted to eat. We froze the meat and that got us through the winter. My Mom prepared the meat to perfection; it was lean and well seasoned. When there were three feet of snow outside, it tasted good. I even killed a deer once. I think I was about twelve. The only thing was, it was a spike and not legal. Legal was a forked horn, minimum. But when I saw that deer in the brush it had horns all over its head. I was excited. I shot it. The 'old heads' told me I had "buck fever." That means I was so intent on the kill I saw what I wanted to see. I knew if I got a buck I would be a man. I had experienced a full dose of the hunter's instinct. But the deer only had one horn. At the time that fact didn't bother me much. We still skinned it and put it in the freezer. I had contributed to our winter's survival. But this is not the only reason why I don't hunt any more. This is: One day the game warden brought us a fawn whose mother had been killed. He knew my Mom could raise anything, calves, sheep, chickens, ducks, turkeys, even raised some baby quail once. She has an incredible maternal instinct. So the game warden brought the fawn to her. She took it and made it a bed in a box and got up in the night to give it regular feedings. I think you can see the rest of the story coming. It grew up to be a pet. We let it go free but it never left. We were its family and the ranch was its home. It was a doe and we named her Squeaky. (Deer make a high pitched squeaking sound.)

Squeaky would come into the house, get on the couch, lie down, and lick the cat. She loved graham crackers. Outside, if you got down on all fours, she would butt heads with you. During hunting season we would tie a big red bow around her neck so people would know she was a pet. It was never much of a problem. She mostly stayed around the house and barns anyway. The dogs just knew she belonged there. The cat was the only one who wished Squeaky would go somewhere else; she got tired of being licked. I would go squirrel hunting—they dug holes in the irrigation ditches and grain sacks—and march along with my rifle under my arm. Squeaky would follow me. This made for sort of an odd sight. The only way I could get her to go home was to climb a tree and sit. She would finally get bored and leave, usually to see if she could find the cat. Squeaky was a beautiful animal. She was so pretty—big ears, big brown eyes and gentle gait—and loving. Now you know why I never hunted again. (Squeaky's gone now but I'm not going to tell you that story because it's too sad and, no, she wasn't shot.)

Men hunt and I understand. They do it with a passion. It is an instinctive passion. The preparation is almost ceremonial: the talking of the hunt, the gathering of the weapons and the sustenance necessary to maintain the hunt. In their minds they are hunting to provide food for their families. Many are in it just for the thrill of the hunt or the trophy head, which becomes the catalyst for many a story, each one getting bigger and better as the years go by. (Most wives are eventually able to relegate these 'trophies' to where they really belong: the barn or garage.)

Real sportsmen are just that, sportsmen. They hunt for the meat and the man fellowship. They keep it a sport, as opposed to a slaughter. Bow hunters come to mind. They have to get close, use stealth and patience. Many of them roll in the dung of the game to disguise their scent. This accomplishes its purpose (until you go home). I know a bow hunter who hunts every year. He never gets anything but he hunts every year just the same. I have this sneaking suspicion he doesn't even want to kill anything. I think he just wants to be there, to know that if he had to he could get game and provide for his family. But he doesn't have to kill so he doesn't. I like this man. So does his family. They just know that each year he has to do his thing. And they also know to get a new can of Lysol for when he comes home.

But the ones who drive their four-wheel-drives—the ones with the chrome roll bars and five spotlights—along the old logging roads, with their guns hanging out the windows, drinking beer and throwing the cans out, they're goons. Just goons. They probably ought to be hunted themselves, for what they do is slaughter. And slaughter eventually destroys the very thing they covet. Better to outlaw this type of behavior.

Back to the reality of hunting. (I had to moralize for Squeaky.) Men do hunt and they do it with both passion and purpose. And they have been doing it ever since the first crop failure, when they had to run down a rabbit in order to satisfy their hunger pangs. Hunting reinforces a very basic instinct in man. The kill isn't always pleasant; it is very aggressive behavior. Hunting is controlled aggression. So men hunt, some for food and some just to know they can. I don't hunt any more, but I understand.

32
FATHERHOOD

Fatherhood is a man thing, by definition. And it is what it has always been: nurturing, protecting, caring, providing for, teaching, and turning loose. None of these things is particularly easy, but each is rewarding in its own way. In this modern day and age, each has taken on some new twists, but they remain as important as ever. As society becomes more complex, the result of crowding and diminishing resources, the nurturing period becomes longer. Because of numerous parental failures society has had to create all sorts of artificial nurturing mechanisms. Some work, but not very well. In that light, fatherhood (and motherhood) are more important than ever. In fact, they are the key to a successful society.

Since this is a book about man things, we'll focus on fatherhood from the man's perspective. Fatherhood is probably the greatest honor a man can have bestowed upon him. It is the culmination of the union of two people who care enough about each other to give life. (That's how it's supposed to be, anyway.) It is also one of man's greatest responsibilities. Men who shirk the responsibility of fatherhood are held in the lowest esteem in man land. It is opportunity as well, to take part in the raising of a productive and happy child. The latter is the truest measure of success in this life.

Nurturing is basic to fatherhood. It is first. To hold your child, warm and dry and content and happy, is to feel life itself. Sure, men have these feelings, much like the mother of the child. They may not always articulate them, but they have them.

A big part of preparing the child for life is about protection. Protection of offspring is one of the most basic instincts. Don't ever get caught between a she-bear and her cubs. And don't ever try to harm a father's child.

Men care deeply about their children. That fact should never be minimized. Men who have experienced caring can more easily pass it on. That is precisely why caring is so important. The child must know that he or she is cared for. That fact needs to be at the core of their being.

Parental caring is also the cause of what I called 'parental frustration,' such as when kids go bad. And kids sometimes do. When you care, it is heartbreaking. But there is only one thing you can do: continue caring. You cannot give up. In the end, the child will draw from the strength of your caring. They may end up doing it over your grave, but they will do it.

Men feel a very deep obligation to provide for their children. Sometimes too deep. They are oftentimes driven to gain wealth. Sometimes they are so driven they lose sight of why. And it is often a downfall, because their children can get lost in the process. The smartest and most successful realize there is a balance between providing for, and leaving time for, children.

Teaching is all important because there is so much to learn. There is learning to get along with others, in school and in life. And learning that hard work and study are the key to any successful endeavor, and that hard work and study are okay, even cool. In sports, we teach about competition, that it isn't just winning but about being out there playing. And losing is a part of playing. But losing is not the worst of things. It is not to be fretted over, but to be built upon. No one wins all the time in life. Teach that early and small failures won't become road blocks; they'll become stepping stones.

Men teach mostly man things, all of the above plus about changing oil, tools, barber shops, crowbars, coiling (often takes a lot of patience), tractors, toy trains, and building stuff. Once I was rotating the tires on my pickup and after I loosened the lug nuts my six year old son would squat down and unscrew them the rest of the way. His hands got dirty and he loved it. He wiped them on his pants like I do. After I would reinstall the wheel he would screw the lug nuts back on by hand, then tighten them with the lug wrench as tight as a six-year-old can tighten. Then he and I would grab the lug wrench together and snug them the rest of the way. Once, while doing this, I heard a click. I turned and it was my neighbor. He had seen the goings on, grabbed his camera, walked across the street and taken our picture. As I turned further he said, "This is how it's supposed to be." As my son and I smiled, the neighbor walked back over to his house. A few days later he brought over a copy of the picture and gave it to us. It is in the family album.

When I was teaching my oldest son to fly, I didn't want to make it too easy for him. I bought an older airplane, one that you have to tinker on to keep going. It was a 1946 Aeronca 7AC Champ, a sweetheart and very basic. It was an excellent airplane in which to teach basic airmanship. You have to work, and care, to keep it working well. I made my son change the oil. Lying on his back, oil dripping down his hands and off his elbows, I asked him, "Is this fun?" I got an unequivocal, "Yeah, this is great Dad!" It was the kind of thing that makes you swell up inside: man feelings.

After teaching, you have to turn loose. Let them leave the nest. It is very difficult. You raised them to be who they are, and to be who they want to be. The only way they can do that is to be let go. Once you let them go, there is no going back. My oldest son called me one day after being involved in a minor fender-bender at a residential street intersection and asked, "What do I do Dad?" I said, "Handle it!" It was tough to say that after all the years of picking him up after he fell, but it had to be said. My parental doubts were later allayed when he told me, "I needed you to say that Dad." It was rather a culmination of fatherhood: a man moment.

I'm still here. I'm still his father. Always will be. But now, someday, he will be a father and he will nurture, protect, care, provide for, teach, and turn loose. I am confident of that. And I am very proud of that. Fatherhood, and loving your wife, should be at the very core of a man's existence. These are man's greatest honors.

33
A MAN DAY WITH BJ

This is about a man day.

I went to visit BJ, my brother-in-law in Texas. His Mom's farm is in Oklahoma. We drove to her farm in BJ's truck with the windows down (they're stuck that way) on a warm spring day. "Air conditioning is for wimps," BJ would say. BJ, his son (age three), my youngest son (age five), and me, bouncing on down the road in man heaven. The little cup BJ uses to spit in was wedged between him and his son. His son knew just how to sit to keep it upright. He probably learned it from practical experience. BJ's in-dash radio speaker doesn't work. He has another speaker that sits on top of the dash, loose wires from it running down to somewhere under the dash. It works. It belted out some fine tunes as we went merrily down the road, tunes like "My Pickup Truck Is My Life" and "Diesel and Dirt in the Morning" and "Gimme Grain in the Breeze and Cows on the Meadow." Real music. It kind of set the tone for the day. I thought we might spend the day tinkering around the farm. I was wrong. I grew up on a farm and I should have known better. But my guard was down. I was visiting. On the farm you tinker in the winter; you work in the spring.

We got to the farm after several lefts and rights on several dirt roads. That's to say I was lost, but I was suitably impressed with BJ's navigational prowess. I mentioned I was impressed and he said, "Hell, you just turn off the main road where the Burma Shave sign fell off the post, take a left at the first juniper tree, go seven miles, right at that big mesquite and then left-right-left past the watering trough." I guarantee you no computer mapping program has that data.

BJ's Mom met us on the porch. From her porch you could see the garden. It was big enough to feed a regiment. I made some comment to that effect. She offered, "Aw, it's nothin'." Nothing for two teams of horses and five men maybe, yet she tended it herself. Nope, this wasn't a tinkering kind of place.

Back into the truck and down more dirt roads we went, by fields and fences and fences and fields, a few trees here and there in the distance, the sky a clear, pale blue. We came upon a tractor sitting in a field. It was a John Deere 4020, I believe, with a big ol' plow attached. The field was partially plowed. We checked the tractor for fuel and oil. It checked out fine. BJ started it. That produced a cloud of smoke and a low rumble. The smoke drifted off into the expansive sky. The rumble remained, suggesting it was time to go to work. BJ said, "Hop on. Gas is here, clutch here and shifter here." My son and I hopped on. I've driven a lot of tractors, but I hadn't driven this particular model before. I found everything where BJ said it was. Put the clutch in, put the shifter in something, gave it some gas, let out the clutch and we were on our way.

Our back was to BJ as we started into the field. When we got to the other end and turned around, I looked back and BJ was gone. I looked around some more and found him. His truck was a speck at the head of a cloud of dust going down the road. The dust trail took a ninety-degree turn, then another turn the opposite direction, then the speck disappeared beyond a rise. The dust slowly dissipated and there we were, John Deere, my son, me, a plow and some soil. Tinkering was out the window; we had work to do. We drove round and round, picking up the corners. The breeze was fairly calm so we didn't have to eat too much dust. We were left here to plow and plow is what we were going to do. And we were going to do it well. Man pride. And we were going do it pretty. Sure you can plow pretty. Men know that. Straight lines and no gaps. Plow pretty and another man might say, "Damn fine job." That's a compliment in man land. Any more than that and the guy might be weird.

We actually finished the field once, but no cloud of dust with a pickup truck in front was in sight. So we started plowing the other way. That's okay. Plowing is soil preparation and more plowing just means the soil is better prepared. Man logic.

As the day wore on we began looking for a canteen hanging on the tractor somewhere. Nothing. Oh well, keep plowing. Our stomachs rumbled a couple of times, but you can't let a little thing like that bother you when you have work to finish. Just turn around and look at the soil, all crumbly and smellin' good. You'll eat later. Remember that garden? You know there's some good stuff be comin' out of there for supper.

We ignored thirst and hunger, and we'd long ago given up on ever seeing BJ again. But our bladders would not be denied. We had to stop the tractor once and take care of business. I went on one rear tire and my son went on the other, out in the middle of nowhere. The spots on the tires just blend in with all the other spots after a while.

The sun was getting low in the horizon, and we were still plowing, when it happened. I saw some dust forming behind a rise. Then over the rise came a speck, spewing more familiar dust. I looked at my watch; it had been seven hours since we last saw that trail of dust. The dust and the pickup made it to the gate in the field about the same time we did. But we weren't about to appear wimpy so we made another round. Then we pulled up to the truck and shut ol' John Deere down. Quiet. It gets real quiet after you shut down a tractor you've been driving all day. Then BJ says, "Damn fine job. Y'all want a Pepsi?" He had one can sitting on the seat of his truck. My son and I made short work of it. Things always taste better when you've earned them. And when you're thirsty as hell.

Back down the road, we all went to the farmhouse. We ate turnips, corn, mashed potatoes, tomatoes, cucumbers, okra, strawberries, and a big ol' slab of Angus beef. Then we said our thanks, piled back in the truck and headed home for Texas. BJ spit, the wind blew through the windows and the loose speaker on the dash belted out "Plowing is Good; Beer is Better" and "Dirt Never Hurt Nobody." And my son and I sank low in our seat and drifted off. I think we were both dreaming the same dream. It was something about spending the day on a tractor at an Oklahoma farm. Except when we woke up it wasn't a dream because we had a slight sunburn to prove it.

Thanks, BJ, for a memorable man day.

34
BBQ

I don't know that barbecue is exclusively a man thing. It is something men enjoy doing. It is sort of like the frosting on a day. You know, the really fun thing of the day you look forward to, the culmination of all your hard work and preparation. A man standing before his barbecue, spatula and fork in hand, is a man in his happy place.

During the winter months we become barbecue deprived. I was recently talking on the phone to my nephew. He lives on the East coast. They had just been through a heck of a winter. I asked him how he was doing. He said he had just finished giving his barbecue a spring tune up. When the sun shined again he was going to be ready. I understood what he was saying. Then he said, "Be sure and put a chapter in your book about barbecue. It's a guy thing." (I believe 'guy thing' is the East coast derivative of 'man thing'.)

Modern barbecue isn't exactly man returning to his primal instincts. The fire burning, the smoke pouring forth, and the meat sizzling are all primal, but today we have elevated it to a pleasant social experience with family and friends. I suppose the original barbecues of several thousand years ago were social events, a celebration of survival. I part from my primal brothers with my push-button ignition and propane fuel tank. The fellowship and the meat remain the same, however.

Barbecue can have far reaching consequences. I was attracted to my wife-to-be by her beauty, intelligence, charm, work ethic, and character . . . and her Dad's ability to barbecue. While dating her I got invited to their house (finally) and, wow, her Dad had one of those big ol' oil drum barbecues. The drum was cut in half, the bottom for the charcoal and the top was the lid. He had a grate of thick steel wire across the middle. He could put a whole bag of charcoal in the bottom of that thing, and usually did. He could also put about twenty-seven hundred steaks or pieces of chicken on it. And he usually did that, too, with four daughters and their various and assorted boyfriends always hanging around the house. Yes, sir, his barbecues were magnificent. I don't know what ever happened to that barbecue, except that it gave way to a gas one when the daughters got married. I can still see him standing there by it, chewing on a cigar, beer in hand, smoke spewing forth, and everyone standing around talking and laughing. His daughter and I have been married twenty-eight years now and he's still barbecuing. That's barbecue legacy.

When you are young in this life you get help from many people along the way and you don't always get to pay them back. As you get older so do they, and many pass on before you are in a position to return their favors. Thus when you get to that point in your life where you can help others, you do. It is sort of a payback for friends and favors past. One day out of the blue, I bought a barbecue for a nephew who is just getting started with home and family. He and I stayed up until midnight putting it together. And we shared a lot of barbecue stories while doing it. He's a hunter so he has put the barbecue to good use. The legacy continues.

Another story about a friend of mine sort of puts the barbecue thing in total perspective. The best day there is, he says, is when, after you've mowed your meadow, you stand before your barbecue, all smokin' and sizzlin', a 'cool one' in hand, and you're looking out over the grass and the Rain Bird sprinkler is going, ". . . sssst . . . sssst . . . sssst . . . sssst." As he says, "It don't get any better." He's right.

Notice I haven't said anything about the food? It's sort of incidental. The techniques and recipes are as varied as mankind itself. Many are family secrets. Many have been passed down for generations. And many are a matter if individual pride. But all are good. Even burned they're good. The issue is the doing as much as the result. And that is the essence of barbecuing. That and all the man stories that take place while the barbecue is happening. Makes me want to go out and fire it up. Soon as this snow stops blowing. . . .

35
BARNS, SHOPS, AND SHEDS

Barns, shops, and sheds are man places. The reasons have been secrets for a long time, but I am about to 'let the cat out of the bag.' I am not sure why I am going to let it out of the bag—I do so with some trepidation—but if we are exploring man things (and we are), we have to explore barns, shops, and sheds.

Barns, shops, and sheds are where men can go and be men. This is *their* place. In them men are serene, confident, comfortable, and at ease. They are themselves. And in them they can do their thing, whatever that thing is. They can do it their way and in their own time. They are boss. In them they are in that magic place called man land. Men love to be in man land.

Some things about barns, shops, and sheds are particularly important. They create man ambiance. Take the floor. It is either wood, dirt, or cement. And in this life of a million linoleum and ten million vinyl patterns and five hundred thousand types and colors of carpet, three choices is nice. It keeps things simple and since men are basically simple creatures, three choices is plenty. Some considerations: wood is great for part of a barn, the part where you store the feed sacks and tack and stuff. It makes a nice hollow 'clomping' sound when you walk on it. When you hear it, it is man music and puts you at peace. You KNOW you are in your place. The balance of the barn is usually dirt, to store hay, equipment, and other barn stuff. That way you can drain various engine oils right on the ground—just like the old days—and cover it up before the OSHA

139

Gestapo comes to take you away. Dirt floors in shops are okay for a while. It just means that you spent all your money on the building itself and you don't have any left over for concreting the floor until next year. Cement is preferred, when you can afford it, because the '67 Corvette restoration you have going can't have any dust on it. It has to be perfect. The cement floor will help you keep it perfect.

All these floors have one thing in common that men love: You don't have to wipe your feet to walk on them. Muddy shoes, muddy boots, grass clippings, oil, grease, whatever on your shoes, it doesn't matter. Just walk on in and stroll around. Oblivious. Men like to be oblivious. Besides, when the accumulated dirt reaches about three feet in depth, you can just hose it out. On a sunny day move all the projects out and hose the floor down. Be quick, however. Leave the cement shop floor uncluttered and unattended too long and you risk a teen-aged roller blade infestation. They love those wide open floors. Veteran men know the name of the game: Hose the shop out once every ten years whether it needs it or not, but be quick about getting all your precious clutter back in there. It is about man-place-preservation.

From the floor let's go to the roof. Some sort of metal is good. The oldest barns had wood shingles, the material of the day. But the darn things just didn't hold up, had to be replaced every fifty years or so. Metal is the name of the game now. You want it to last a very long time and metal does. You want to work in your shop, not on it. And you want to be able to hear the rain on it. Metal is especially good for that; you can hear the rain loud and clear. Rain is a superb justification for you to be in the shop, and not weeding the flower beds like you promised. Rain on the roof is an excuse to finish the rumble seat installation on the Model A instead. With a metal roof and a good ear you can, in your mind, make a drizzle sound like a downpour. That way you can keep right on working on the Model A. Oblivious. Happy.

Now that we've covered barns, shops, and sheds from bottom to top, let's get to what really makes them man places: the inside. You know what makes them so cool? They are undecorated. At least not with anything that you buy just to decorate, unless it is that golf bag lamp you won at the tournament five years ago. It only made it two steps inside the house before it was ordered out. Actually shops are decorated. But they are man decorated. There is a huge difference between decorated and man decorated. Decorated means having to wipe your feet; man decorated means a gathering of man stuff. Like ropes and wires and new tools and old tools and golf bag lamps. Pure man stuff. It is not so much decoration as accumulation. And it is all yours, a monument to projects past, a palate for projects future, and a shelter from that cluttered and confused world that exists outside man land. Shops are made by men, for men, and of men. So are barns and sheds. They are man heaven.

The magnificent ambiance of barns, shops, and sheds sets the tone for what takes place in there: man work. Man work is fixing, creating, restoring, building, and talking of fixing, creating, restoring and building. A good mix for when you are in your shop is 20% contemplating, 50% doing, and 30% talking. A good shop, a good rain, and a good project are a darn sight cheaper than some mumbo-jumbo therapy, and a heck of a lot more effective. Not to mention more fun.

Barns, shops, and sheds are where men go to be happy. Stop by some time. Hang out. Get dirty. Take off your watch and stay awhile.

36
THINGS MEN CAN'T DO

I hope I didn't scare you with that blank page by implying I couldn't think of anything men can't do. I can. I just didn't want it to appear too easy. This is man pride. There are things men can't do, and I'm going to tell you about some of them. But I am hoping this turns out to be a short chapter.

Men can't grocery shop. I know this from personal experience. Whenever I am sent to the grocery store my success ratio for getting the right thing is less than fifty percent, even with a list. Even with a very detailed list. But, dangit, it is not altogether my fault. The list, which has gotten ever more detailed over the years given my less than fifty percent success ratio, might say, 'croutons, large green box, garlic flavor, red and white checked top, about $1.85, get two boxes.' The list does not tell me which aisle it is on, and that is a problem. There are five million aisles in the grocery store. I know there are five million because I walked down every one of them trying to find the dang croutons. (I darn sure wasn't going to ask where they were; that would not be manly.) It is a jungle of plethora. And the lights in the grocery store are ten million candlepower. And there are whirling cardboard figures, rotating beacons, leaning towers of pizza, and a laser light show over by the tomatoes. I am intimidated. By the time I find the croutons, I am tired. Fatigue influences my judgment. My better judgment tells me to get the hell out of this place but spousal loyalty makes me stay. I persevere.

The crouton section. There's an Empire State building of crouton boxes on display. Choices. Way too many choices. I finally find the green boxes with the red and white checked top. I use the extension ladder provided to get to them. There are onion flavor, kiwi flavor, no flavor, dirt flavor, onion and kiwi flavor, but no garlic flavor. No, wait! There's one! Behind the big onion/kiwi box. But it only costs 95¢. It is not a very big box. Probably why it is only 95¢. And there is only one box. The list says get two boxes. Can't. There's only one. So I pick it up. I go to check out. This is Thursday. From the looks of the line I won't get home until Friday. Fortunately I miscalculated. I get home Thursday.

She asks, "Get the croutons?"

"Yup."

"I wanted two boxes."

"There was only one."

"I needed the larger box."

"That was the only size they had."

"You'll have to go back to another store."

"Aaaarrrgh!" With the incorrect number of boxes and the wrong size box, my success ratio has plummeted to a miserable forty percent. It's no wonder women live longer than men.

"Why is it that men can't ever get the right thing?"

"It's a genetic flaw. Four thousand more years of evolution and we'll get it right. Promise."

Nope, men can't grocery shop. Fortunately, because of our genetic flaw, we don't get asked to very often.

Men cannot do laundry. The way it is supposed to be done, anyway. Too many choices again. Whites with whites and colors with colors. I've got that down. But is gray a white or a color? And how about the striped things? Is the red and white striped sweater red or is it white? Something about 'separates' in here, too. I know about 'separate' but not about 'separates'. And there is much ado about cold water or hot water or warm water or gentle cycle or normal cycle or normal/gentle cycle, not to mention the dad-gum water level. Or how much soap to use. Or whether it goes in first, last, or in the middle. And my cotton boxer shorts are colored so why do they go in with the whites? There is not only too much to know, there is great risk. If that red and white striped sweater comes out pink and the size of a glove, you are in some kind of big trouble. No, men can't do laundry. I would rather totally restore a derelict Model A. That makes sense. And it would be a lot easier than doing the laundry, too.

Okay, that's it. Those are the only two things men can't do. "Uh, *right!*", I can hear one half of the population all across America saying. Okay, okay, I'll think of something else. . . .

. . . I'm still thinking. . . .

37
TINKERING

Tinkering. This is a man thing. Heck, it is a man art form. It is where you can spend a whole bunch of time looking like you are doing something yet accomplish nothing. That's the beauty of it. You are not supposed to accomplish anything. You are just supposed to do stuff, stuff that is no big deal. But stuff that is fun to do. And because it is no big deal and it is fun, it relaxes you. Puts you at peace. Happy. That is why men tinker.

The reason it is an art form is because it is not easy to do. You kind of have to develop a technique, then hone it to perfection. It takes a while to be able to do that. There are a few good tinkerers under the age of twenty-five, but most are over fifty.

The biggest danger in tinkering is taking what you do too seriously. You must guard against that. Take it too seriously, i.e., start thinking you have to get it done today or what you are doing is real important, then what you are doing becomes work. Tinkering must never be work. Work ruins the ambiance of tinkering. You must never be in a hurry. Tinkering has to be done slow. Slow . . . down. W-a-y down. That is the key to successful tinkering. It is also why you can tinker so long. Time has no place in what you are doing. And, in this day and age, it is wonderful when time does not matter.

Usually we tinker in a garage or shop. For hours. Some may ask what we could possibly be doing in the shop all those hours. The answer is, "Tinkering." Tinkering consists of many things, as many things as there are men and as individual as every man. But I can give you some examples so you will have some idea what has been going on in the shop all those days and nights and hours: We take some-thing and we take some tools and we work on it. Just work on it. We don't have to finish it by some time. We don't have to finish it at all. It doesn't matter how much time we have to spend not finishing it either. We plod along, happily perfecting the art of tinkering.

Tinkering often includes doing things that we said we would get to someday. Like that worn ratchet on the boat winch. The old ratchet still works—sort of—and we've had the new one for some time now. But we wanted to save it for when we didn't have to do it in a hurry. We wanted to do it while tinkering. Or the carburetor on the old lawn mower engine. We might take it off and clean it out. That would be great tinkering. It is not too strenuous, we get to use a lot of different tools, and it would take a while with all those little parts. It's November so we won't need the carburetor until May. Taking five months to do a thirty minute job is tinkering perfection. Or we might just work on a piece of wood for the wine rack we have been promising for a year. Like hardwood. Oak hardwood. Smells good. Feels good. And it is expensive so we are careful with it. There is a lot of perfection involved; we don't want to make any wrong cuts. A hardwood project slows you down. That is why it is so good for tinkering. Or we might fiddle with the upholstery on the Model A. We have been tinkering on it for three years now. We have a couple more years to go. No hurry. Tinker on it when you can. For as long as you can.

Tinkering for three hours and finishing about the time the football game starts will get you a Ph.D. in tinkering.

Some people swear by therapy. I swear by tinkering.

38
THE MEADOW

The meadow was a magical place. I didn't realize it at the time, but it was. I did know it was my boy place. It lay between our house and the barn. It had hills on one side and a river on the other. It was a broad expanse of various types of grasses with clover and cow-pies mixed in. Both of the latter were okay. The clover was cause for hunting the elusive four leaf one and it was the cows that kept the meadow mowed. Each had their rights.

The meadow was magical because only good things happened there. I could go there and it was always happiness I found. I could be a running back carrying a football, dodging cow-pies with great swiftness, tripping myself to fall down and get up again slowly with great courage to the roar of the crowd that was the hill and the river. Second down. Cut right this time. Tackled again. Always, always get back up. I could do that all day. Touching the barn was a touchdown. I touched the barn a lot. Or I could be a gymnast and run and tumble and handspring and tumble some more and hear the roar of the wind's approval. Or I could throw a baseball in the air and hit it with the bat and watch it soar into the blue. The wall I hit it over was always just in front of wherever the ball landed. "Another home run!" I would say to myself as I trotted around the cow-pie bases.

I was never alone on the meadow. I had my imagination, my spirit, and Brucie. Brucie was my collie dog, my big ol' gentle, tail-wagging, tongue-hanging-out, smiling, always there, always happy collie dog. When I was in football land he would run beside me. When I got "tackled" he would sit at the line of scrimmage until the next down. Then we would go again. When I tumbled, he would run along side. I sensed he wanted to tumble, too, but he never did. In baseball land Brucie was the key. I would throw the ball up and hit it and he would chase it down, pick it up and bring it back to me. Then I would hit the slobber-ball again. I always figured if I could hit a slobber-ball I could hit anything. Each time, Brucie brought the ball back a little slower and was a little more reluctant to drop it at my feet. Finally, after about the tenth home run, he would go get the ball (he *always* got it) but on the return trip he would veer off about halfway back, plop down, drop the ball between his feet and look at me. It was time for the seventh inning stretch.

The seventh inning stretch was great. I would go where Brucie was, lay down on my back, put my head on his flank, and we would talk and dream. Sometimes we would just watch the puffy white clouds float by. Or, if it was 2:10 P.M., a lone Douglas DC-3 always droned overhead and we would watch it from horizon to horizon, the deep-throated rumble of the radial engines striking a chord in my heart. I think sometimes I may have gone to sleep in the peace. Brucie must have, too, because he never moved until I did. What a friend he was, never complained, never criticized, always listened, always fun. No one ever had to explain to me what friendship was. Brucie had already taught me. He was a big part of the meadow's magic.

Sometimes my Dad would put me on the tractor on the meadow. Ford model 8N. And I do mean "put me on" it. He would just sit me on the seat; I could steer but I couldn't reach the pedals. He would put me on it, put it in the lowest gear, get it going, then he would get off and I would steer all over the meadow. Child cruelty? Hardly. I loved it. Behind the tractor was a heavy screen. I would drag it around and break up the cow-pies. Wherever they were, and they were everywhere, that is where I steered. It helped to fertilize the whole field by "spreading the wealth," so to speak. When my Dad figured the field was finished he would walk up alongside the tractor, swing up on it and push in the clutch. It would stop and I would get off with a great feeling of accomplishment and head for whatever was next. I still love tractors, especially Ford 8N's.

The meadow had bees and butterflies and gnats and ants. I spent a lot of time marveling at what it was they did. They were all so industrious and purposeful. That is a good way to be. I never wondered why they did what they did. It didn't seem to matter. That they were doing it was good enough for me. And that they did it so well was almost motivational. No, it *was* motivational. Nature's a good example of how to live.

Through all this, the two milk cows kept their peace and their place on the meadow. Green grass makes good milk. They would munch, lay down, chew their cud, do their thing. They shared the meadow nicely. That is what made it so great. It was a beautiful place and we all shared it equally and nicely.

That is what the world needs, more meadows and less graffiti. Every kid should have a meadow where they can go and be "alone," safe, dream and just be. A meadow is a great start on life.

39
THE LAKE

Ah, the lake. It offers a veritable cornucopia of man things. The family goes there every year for vacation. There is a rustic cabin on the lake's edge, with a real knotty pine interior and a view of the surrounding mountains. The air is crisp and clean. No phones. No TV. No radio. No 586 SX with a 27 gigabyte hard drive and 1000 megabytes of RAM with 2700 pre-installed software titles and a super-duper-deluxe-extra-special-outdated-next-month VGA Yπ monitor either. The answering machine is, get this, a note pad. In other words, no artificial sounds or inputs of any kind. Just pure and natural solitude. Heaven. It does have running water, a flushing toilet, and a gas stove and fridge. We are not totally Neanderthal. Something else the lake has: damn few people. It puts rush hour traffic and crowded shopping malls deep in the recesses of your mind, where they belong.

But first we have to get there, and that is where the 'cornucopia of man things' begins. The cabin is far away; you have to prepare to get there and plan for being there. To prepare you have to gather some tools, like the shovel and the axe. And the lantern. And you have to tinker on the boat, check that the oars are on board and all the ropes are coiled. And, of course, for the long trip you have to change the oil on your truck. Fresh oil is important for any journey. We do all this stuff—this man stuff—in the shop. And we do it in blue jeans and a T-shirt and well-worn but comfortable boots. There is a lot of man stuff going on here and that is just mighty fine.

My wife plans the groceries. I could do it, but I think she is afraid that if I do, the variety would be lacking. A couple weeks of biscuits by morning and hamburgers by evening wears on her. Variety is okay. Not absolutely necessary, but okay. The kids seem to think variety is necessary, at least after the first couple of days. Whatever. As long as I get to BBQ from time to time. . . .

The journey involves even more man things, like hooking up the boat to the pickup. The pickup has a low, eager-to-go-to-the-lake rumble, and it sets you up high for the back-roads journey. It primes you. You are ready and it is ready. Don't forget to load up the family.

Down the road you go, man philosophy on your mind. "Get one with nature." Banter, in your mind, with the log truck drivers, "Hey, move that piece of crap truck over so I can get by." The truck driver counters, in his mind, "Up yours." Maybe even signs you with a single digit hand signal. You both laugh. It's a great day to be alive.

We pull over at the roadside cafe. The cafe sits in a canyon beside a rushing creek. The waitress comes up with coffee. She is real, and likes families. We all order big stuff . . . eggs, hotcakes, sausage, the works. It is traditional. It is also good.

From there we make a quick run across the road to the hardware/fishin' store to "man shop." Get an extra wick for the lantern. "Hey, let's get this fishin' lure for Aaron's man pack." Men can't have too many lures. Okay, we're outta here. "See ya later, Bud." Bud says, "You guys have fun." The screen door bangs closed.

Back in the truck and back down the road we go, all jabbering, excited, and happy. We turn off the pavement onto the dirt road. We're gettin' real now. No asking for directions here; no one to ask. We navigate by the sun, the shadows, the canyons and the peaks . . . and by the only road there is to the lake.

Around the last bend in the road and, through a gap in the trees, there it is. Serene. Calm. Blue. Inviting. Five thousand feet above sea level. The family makes a pact. Don't tell anyone where this place is. More man philosophy: "No place is so beautiful that it can't be ruined by too many people."

Open up the cabin. It is a little musty, but it freshens quickly with all the windows open. Unload. Stuff goes here and there. Food goes on the counter. Put the boat in the lake and tie it to the dock. Walk back up to the cabin, turn around and look out over the lake. Take in a deep breath and let it out slow. We are here. The family gathers, all feeling the same thing. We don't say much. We reflect. It has been a pretty good year. We are healthy, happy, and there is a lot of love in this family. We are not rich. We are not famous. We are just here. Yeah, it has been a good year.

At the lake clocks and watches are prohibited. Time is measured by the sun, if it is measured at all. Fishin' is in the early morning, followed by a big mountain breakfast, and floating and swimming and hiking in the afternoon. Maybe we work in an afternoon nap now and then, drifting off under the shade of a tall pine tree, with no thoughts on our minds other than the peace around us.

Sometimes some of our very best friends visit us at the lake. Like Miriam and Bob. She has the sweetest disposition West of the Mississippi, and he is the educated bombast. He quotes Yeats and Frost by the fireside and has a heart of gold. It all adds up to life at its very best.

I brought you to the lake. I would like to leave you here, end this book right now. But life isn't like that. No place is forever. No mood is forever. A general feeling of happiness *is* something that is within our reach. We only have to know the things that make us happy, then pursue them.

When I am not at the lake, I work. I move dirt with my tractor, tinker on the Model A, change the oil, banter with the good ol 'boys, dream about my dump truck, admire my crowbar, coil the hoses, eat meat loaf sandwiches, have strong opinions about some things, watch football, tell fishin' lies at the barber shop and try to be as good a husband and father as I can.

I can try to write like I have all the answers. But I don't. I do know this: Forget all the politically correct window dressing; it is okay to be a man doing man things. Especially at the lake.

40
MODERN MAN

Sometimes you see men in suits, working in offices, living in suburbs, and farming out every known man task to others. There are men like that. But that does not mean they are always happy doing it. My guess is if they could, they would be out doing man things. I bet they dream about it a lot.

Guess what a man does when he can get away from it all: He goes fishin.' And camping. And he puts on his blue jeans and T-shirt and gets dirty. And, if there was a "Plowers Anonymous" (coming soon, to a location near you!), he would go there, too.

How do I know all this? I just do. Basic man things burn deep in all of us. Take the lawyer who just cashed it all in to be a train conductor, on his own train. Or the corporate executive who gave it all up to open a hardware store in a log building in Montana. And the highly paid, big city physical therapist who quit his hectic life style to open a donut shop in Small-town, U.S.A. These are true stories. And there are a lot more just like them. A return to the basics. And they all own old pickup trucks, change their own oil, man banter, have crowbars, build fences, have coveralls, admire Jim's compressor, love their wives, and otherwise are happy just being men doing man things.

These guys have a head start. When this society gets going so fast that it can no longer sustain itself, when we use up our last non-renewable resource, when the information age becomes information overload, man will have to return to the basics. He will return to working with his hands and his heart, to caring, and to honesty. Men will return to man things. We will all be good ol' boys. And women will still know in their hearts that, given clear guidance and perfect instruction, we will still bring home the wrong box of croutons from the grocery store.

ORDER FORM

———————

For additional copies of *Man Things*, contact your local bookstore or send $12.95 plus $2.00 shipping and handling per book to:

CASCADE PUBLISHING
PO Box 4598
Salem, OR 97302

Name: _____

Address: _____

City, State, Zip: _____

Phone: _____

INTERNET WEBSITE:
http://www.mavbooks.com/bookstore/man_things.htm